Living 4 God

Will I Prevail?

LmHt

ISBN 978-1-64458-899-4 (paperback)
ISBN 978-1-64458-900-7 (digital)

Christian Faith Publishing, Inc.
832 Park Avenue
Meadville, PA 16335
www.christianfaithpublishing.com

All scriptures are from the King James Version of the Holy Bible. Some are direct quotes, while others are paraphrased.
Most of the scriptures used in my poetry and writings are paraphrased and used from the King James Version of the Holy Bible.

Printed in the United States of America

I dedicate this book to Denise, my sister-in-law, who has inspired me to keep writing from beginning to end. Thanks, Denise. I love you.

"Circles do not end, but time does."

This book is a true story, but names have been changed.

All of my poetry is written as expressions of my life experiences.

Two other poets that I know who love the Lord have agreed to submit some of their works in this book. Read, enjoy, and be blessed.

I am also putting together an audiobook where you will be able to hear the dramatization of my poetry.

Introduction

The spirit (which is inside of me) and the flesh (which is on the outside of me) are at war, one against the other. Read it for yourself in the Bible, in Romans 7:13–17.

The title of this book—*Living4God: Will I Prevail?*—is so chosen because of the daily struggles in life.

Struggling within and fighting without, where is the truth? My worries? My doubts?

My dad was once a very vibrant and expressive man, but now he has been diagnosed with dementia, which has reduced him into this numb, inactive, expressionless man who now appears before my very eyes. Sometimes he is aggressive, sometimes with hallucinations, other times with abusive and offensive language, sometimes with garbled speech, and oft times with no speech at all.

Do I want to claim what is before my eyes, what I am now seeing versus the dad I once knew? Do I want to claim the deterioration, the confusion, the boy trapped inside of a man, the soul that is so lost within himself? No! Not now or ever do I want to claim what appears before my eyes with my dad. Why?

Because it was when he started to pay attention to the Word of God that I noticed that this thing seems to have come upon him. An attack? A trial? Or perhaps maybe just payback? Things that life put out. Things that we put in. Where…does it…all end?

Praying without ceasing. This is the key that unlocks the door for the blessings of God to be poured into our lives. But how many of us are able to pray without ceasing? We often go right back into our "flesh" modes or states. The things that we have learned, our past behaviors if you will, the habits that we so depend on. And then, once we've stayed there a while and wrestled with the things that have vexed us, we remember and remind ourselves that we must repent. That's my struggle with this walk. And this struggle is real, but it is also very good. Will? I do have the will to prevail. A "will" to struggle against the sin that is in me. I want to holler. I want to scream. But the Holy Ghost that lives on the inside of me is the real person in me that is unseen yet keeps me calm. That's why I am thankful, ever so grateful, and always wanting to learn about the things of God. I love God, and I love people. Now, I don't like all the actions of people. As a matter of fact, I hate the very garments that we possess, for they are stained with sin. Yes, I hate this garment of flesh that I am wrapped up in, it makes me think about Romans 7:19 and see myself doing the things that I hate. And the good that I want to do, I find myself not doing it. And from this, I surmise with confidence, to strive for the good that is in me. I work for it. I long for it. I call out to it. I tell myself to lean on and trust God for it. Then…*it* happens.

And because *it* happens, my purpose in writing this book, as is also my purpose for everything in life, is to point you to the God of all creation. The one who is the very source of all things that exist, and all things consist because of him. But in order to point you into His direction, please allow me to be as truthful as I can about my walk with God. And in order to be truthful, I must be somewhat vulnerable. And in being somewhat vulnerable, I must be somewhat transparent. And in being somewhat transparent, I expose my weaknesses. And in exposing my weaknesses, I allow for someone to trample upon my feelings and say things like, "Aha! I knew [this or that] about her. I knew she wasn't any good." For I know that is the way people behave at times, 'cause I've done it myself until I became aware of the hurt that I could cause others (even when it's done behind their backs), and the consequences that hinder my growth into the person that God wants me to be, so I say to that somebody, "Be careful. Do you really believe that you are as bad as me? If you can tear me down, then I must say that you are just as bad as me. 'Cause I have torn down others and am cable of doing the same to you."

As a matter of fact, we as human beings love to talk about each other. It makes us feel better about ourselves. We often tell ourselves and others, *At least I'm not as bad as her or him*, but in actuality we really are. And that's the whole truth and nothing but the truth. We are most pitiful, because in the next breath, we are praising God, and now we are sanctimonious. Okay, okay, I am talking about me. Not you. See, I don't mind talking about me. Why? Because my struggle is real. I help myself in these writings because I've seen the good, the bad, and the ugly in me. Oh, and by the way, I'm not talking about outward physical appearance. And let the truth also be told, that isn't going to last anyway. It's so temporary. I wonder why we get caught up, so hard up, for looks and appearances. Oh yeah, that's right, we have to be appealing to others. We are afraid of: being lonely, alone, and winding up being by ourselves. I've even had people tell me, "Girl, you don't want to be alone." Well, I did. I wanted to be alone with God. To learn more about what He had to say. What He wanted me to do. But people wouldn't allow it. They got in the way. Oh, I mean my personal family and my personal friends. They didn't mean harm. They thought that they were looking out for my best interests. They meant well. Like the times when I've intervened in some dangerous situations.

On one particular day, I was coming down the stairs and on my way to school, when I noticed my neighbor standing in the doorway, muttering to herself, "My, my, my, my, terrible, terrible, terrible…"

I interrupted and said, "What's the matter?"

She pointed toward the big glass window pane of the big wooden front door and said, "Look. Those kids are beating that man."

"What…?" I followed her finger to see what was going on. I looked, and there in the vacant lot across the street were a gang of children who looked to be teenagers. They had sticks, bottles, and stones and they were throwing, and they were beating up on a man who was lying on the ground in a ball, who seemingly was trying to protect himself as best as he could. As I looked on for a couple of seconds, which seemed to be minutes, I said in a soft voice, not really talking to her but more to myself, "What…I've got to get out there."

Her voice seemed anxious, and she was somewhat apprehensive as she grabbed me by the arm. My thoughts were interrupted as she said, "No, no, don't go out there, I've called the police."

As I gently removed her hand from my arm and began to open the door, I said, "I've got to go." As I stepped forward and down the stairs, I prayed, "Father in Jesus's name, I am going." Then I moved quickly forward, down the stairs, across the street, and into the vacant lot, praying as I moved. The children saw me coming, and they began to run back and away from the man and away from me. So as I kept coming forward, they kept moving backward. As I moved, I also prayed. When I got to where the man was, I noticed that he was not moving. I called out gently, "Sir…" I waited a second or two for any response, any movement. There was none, so I called out again, "Sir…" Still no answer, no response. I looked up, and the kids were coming back with their sticks, bottles, and stones. I stood fast where I was. And I prayed, "Okay, Father, I am standing here. The blood of Jesus be over me." The kids started moving backward again, but they did not leave. They were watching me from the other end of the lot (which was about forty feet away, near the alley where the lot ended). So as I stood, I prayed, and other adults began to come out from their houses and stand with me. 1…2…then 3…and more…until there were enough of us to form a half circle around the man. The children then left, and finally after about three minutes or so, which seemed like an hour or so, a fire truck came on the scene. Struggles within, fighting without.

Poem: Love Makes a Difference

And you say love will cause me to do right.
Struggling within, fighting without.
Where is the truth? As I worry and doubt…
Confusion, delusions of grandeur, lies, hypocrisy, gossip,
debauchery, strife—these are pieces of my life.
And did I fail to mention, you told me,
love would make a difference.

What kind of differences should I see?
You say, "Love your enemy and help your friends."
Does this love have an end?
Give to them that have and those that don't.
They can't give back what I want.
They are the sick, the substance abused, the lame,
the maimed, the alcoholic, the misconstrued, and the least pursued.

You say the return of my labor will multiply
when I least expect it—surprise! And love will cause me
to do right. You tell me about this love, but
where is the proof you're speaking of?

You say, "Love them that cuss you."
I think I need a reminder there.
"Love them that wrong you."
I can't seem to find her (my patience) anywhere.
"Love them that despitefully use you."
How long can I stand under this kind of pressure?
Will my bitter heart show an illusion or a mere appearance?
Where do I get this love?

And you say love makes a difference.
Sacrifice? Who, me? Who will help me during…my plight,
in my distress…in my fight for wrong and right?

You say, "Love God."
I say, "Why?"
Because He says, "Love me with all your might."
So I say, "I love you, Lord." But then you question,
telling me I failed to see the real light, the sacrifice, the charge,
the ONE who was guiltless, who was actually sentenced.
You asked me. Now I'll ask you, "Does love still
make a difference?"

There's a man sitting with a sign, on the road.
Do I close my eyes, turn my head, and walk on by?
You say, "Show me love." It's time to give the last I have
to another one who can't give back. Will I pass, or will I fail?
This test is now. Will I prevail?

You say, "Now is the time for salvation,
but not quite the time for recompense." And you continue
to say to me, "Love makes a difference."

You say God wants all of me. I say, "Why"? ... God? ...
I can't ... see...Lazarus, begging on the side.
I want to say, "That isn't God." But...you...beg to differ,
and tell me instead, "Love makes a difference."

You say,
"You can't love God and not love people."
It just doesn't work like that.
The love of God has an abundance of grace.
That grace will never slack.
It rains on the just, the unjust, the poor.
It reaches the high, the low.
The grace of God is wrapped in love,
with salvation for all who ask. Therefore,
serve God consistently, diligently, effectively, fervently,
and with reverence, 'cause love makes a difference.

Differences? Didn't you know…
that people can speak in tongues and do miracles
and tell God with sincerity, "We love you, Lord."
But…love shows.
People are drawn to our charismatic ways,
and crowds a-follow, but it's still about us.
We won't take time to help a brother, a sister,
for they are beneath us. We won't take time
to reach out, lend a helping hand. We're the preacher,
the pastor, the teacher. Let someone else help.
Let the congregation give. Let them pick 'em up.
We're too big. We're too proud. We're doing our
number one preference. But you still tell us,
"Love makes a difference."

You say, "No longer live for yourselves,
but allow God's will for
love, joy, and peace to be your makeup,
long-suffering and gentleness to be your wake up.
To goodness and faith, meekness and temperance.
Then you'll show the fruit of the Spirit, for
love makes a difference.

You look to see, whom we sit with at the dinner,
whom we call on when we're tempted,
which sick do we visit when we can.
Where are the clothes for the naked?
Where is the name brand…

Which of the hungry people will we feed?
Which of the prisoners will we see?
Where is the sacrifice of our time?
How do we spend the dollar, the dime?
Eat! Drink! And be merry, while we build up barns
and store up treasures…
Someone's crying, someone's hurt, in

pain, sorrow, suffering, and sin, asking,
"Where's my splendor, and what's my end?"
While Godly sorrow is working repentance,
it's LOVE that really makes the difference!

> "Beloved, let us love one another: for love is of God." (1 John 4:7, KJV)

Chapter 1
What Is Promotion

The classroom was so big, and we were so little. We had to sit up straight in our chairs, fold our hands on our desk, and not speak unless we raised our hands. And then we had to wait until we were acknowledged by the teacher. I never raised my hand. I just sat quietly and listened. And tried hard not be seen or heard as much as possible. After all, here I was, a little country girl in the big ol' Windy City. Our family had moved here from the South about two years ago. I was the fourth of eight children, and Mother didn't have a lot of money. Most of our clothes were bought from the rummage sale stores. That's what the thrift/secondhand stores were called back in the day. We were always clean though—Mother made sure of that. But it was still kind of embarrassing because the majority of the kids wore new clothes, especially during the first few weeks of school. Man, I could not wait until those first weeks were over. Then, I thought in my little mind, and only then could I blend in with the other students.

Another reason I tried hard not to raise my hand, I remember Mother saying to us, "Hush, girl, hush your mouth." She often stressed, like many of the other older adults, that children were to be seen and not heard. This saying stuck with me for a long time, even into my adult life and while raising my own children. It wasn't until later that I learned that people need to express themselves—of course, in appropriate ways. It is unfortunate that this lesson was not learned earlier in my life. Another reason I never raised my hand was because our teacher might have been a little prejudiced. I noticed when someone of my color would raise their hand to give an answer, most times they were overlooked and a Hispanic child would be acknowledged. So after all these barriers, why would I bother to raise my hand or even try to give an answer or a thought?

The school's population consisted mostly of African Americans (we called ourselves Negros in those times)—about 60 percent African Americans; then Hispanics, about 35 percent; and lastly whites, about 5 percent. The white population was the faculty. We African American children didn't talk much to the Hispanic children, and they didn't talk much to us. We just went to school together. Most of the Hispanics were trying to move out of the community, and more African Americans were moving in. Anyway, here I was in the second grade. I didn't know that I had a thick accent, a "country" one at that. Example, instead of chicken, I would say "sheken." So here I am, sitting with my hands folded, being obedient and listening to the teacher, when another teacher entered the classroom, spoke quietly to our teacher, and passed her a slip of paper. Our teacher then spoke to the class and said, "When you hear your name called, please get up and go with Mrs. Jaye. You will be in her class every day at this time, for two hours, and then you are to come back here before class is dismissed. Mrs. Jaye is going to help some of you learn how to talk because some of you need to learn how to speak better." You could hear a snicker or two from the students, and the teacher that had come into our class looked at our teacher as if to say, "Really?"

So Mrs. Saye, our teacher, kind of put her head down and looked at the list and started calling out names. "Millicent Hinton," I heard my name called, so I got up and followed Mrs. Jaye and two other students from our class into the large gray hallway, which was empty at this time except for the other students who were waiting for Mrs. Jaye. There were about ten of us in all. We were escorted down the now quiet and empty hallways, down the long flight of stairs. *Clang, clang, clickety clang, clang...*I could hear the sounds of the heels on our shoes as they hit the cemented gray floors that we walked on, in a single file, following Mrs. Jaye as she led the way. No one spoke a word. The stillness in the air as we moved and the sounds of our heels hitting the floors as we marched forward made me think about the story of the Pied Piper (a book I had read from the school library).

I imagined the sounds of our shoes as the song piped on the flute as the children followed the piper out of town and into—my thoughts were interrupted when we stopped abruptly at a small door. Mrs. Jaye pulled out a key and opened the door to the classroom. Then she stood to the side, holding the door open with her foot, as she waved us, one by one, into the small classroom. As we entered, she nodded her head and said, "Welcome, please have a seat anywhere you like." As I went into the classroom, I noticed that the desks were arranged close together and were in a circle facing each other. I grabbed the first chair I saw. It didn't matter anyway. I couldn't sit in the back or middle and hide. So I just sat down, folded my hands, and waited to see what was to happen next.

It was surprising to see Mrs. Jaye take a seat right in the midst of us. Then she welcomed us again into her class and had us introduce ourselves to one another. We were made to feel so very comfortable, and our time with Mrs. Jaye became a fun time that we looked forward to. So every school day for two hours, we were escorted out of our regular class and taken into Mrs. Jaye's class. The hours were not spent in vain. We learned a lot and had so much fun learning. Mrs. Jaye was one of the best teachers I've ever had. Maybe I'm being prejudiced because this was where I learned to express my thoughts through poetry and writing. It was in this class that we were taught how to use words in role play, tongue twisters, and poetry and how to write short stories. We didn't even realize at the time that something was wrong with us—Mrs. Jaye made it all so fun. We didn't even realize that we were learning. She had her own unique style, and it worked because we learned and learned well. This was also where I learned how to perform on the stage. She would have us to do skits, tongue twisters, and poetry on the stage, in front of lots of people. And we performed with excellence because Mrs. Jaye would have it no other way. There was no half doing anything with her. We had to go all out, and she made sure we were well prepared.

Being onstage frequently increased our popularity with the other students and teachers. We were well known throughout the school. Mrs. Jaye also made sure that we didn't fall behind in our other subjects. She would also teach us math and spelling. So what could have been a disaster turned out to be a blessing—bigger than what I could have imagined at that time. Poetry has helped me throughout my life to express feelings that I know I would not have ordinarily expressed. Even to this day, I think that I am still somewhat quiet as a person. I don't talk a lot unless it is something that I am very passionate about. So here was this little country girl with her funny Southern accent, who had trouble enunciating words, who was now able to formulate words into rhymes, poems, plays, and short stories. I call it my promotion.

Poem: What Is Promotion?

A higher position or rank in life,
an act of furtherance, a cause or an aim.
An upgrade, elevation, a higher state of mind,
an advancement, a step-up, a setup.
Promotion can be unpredictable at times,
like
when the boss raised up another
and sat you down, when it was you
who stayed long hours and did all the work,
while she joked around.
She got the promotion that you should've gotten.
Talk about promotion,
yeah…you were hot!
The job got done, and you got what?
Told to sit down and told to cool out,
wait your turn…
'cause all the promotions are over and done!

Then what…There is false promotion.
That will elevate your mind. Substances, such as drugs,
that will make you feel fine
and take you to this temporary state
that's in your mind.
A short-lived high, a deceptive thing,
one you'll chase again and again.
It'll then let you down into reality, where
there is no more family and no more friends.
Everything then is just formality
until you can get that substance again.
Going around in circles that'll never end.
That's a promotion that never wins.

Then promotion can happen from the inside out.
A new creation, created in Christ.
Transformation from dark to light.
This type of promotion is out of sight!

Promotion can be great or small,
but true promotion brings glory to God.
So if your promotion doesn't happen
in the way you thought it should have.
Then there is promotion…in the ever after.
When the trumpet does sound, and
the dead does rise,
and we'll be changed in the blink of an eye,
and
we'll meet the LORD in the sky!
No more waiting on the boss,
hoping and yearning with new expectations
and still missing out.
For JESUS has been given a name
highly exalted above all.
At the name of JESUS, every knee will bow.
Promotion comes not from the east or the west.
Neither does it come from the south.
So if you receive your promotion in the
here and now,
remember, God is judge of all.
He is King of kings and Lord of lords.
He has your best interest in the center of HIS heart.
He knows what you're made of inside and out,
and He doesn't set you up and then let you fall!

Chapter 2
Too Young to Be Fast

What do you know, at the age of eleven I was molested by an uncle—who would have ever thought? Not a kid—not me! I remember being so scared, but at the same time my little mind was working overtime, trying hard to find a way out of that mess! My two brothers and I were at home. We had missed school that day because Mother had to attend to some business and my little brother, Joey, was ill. Someone had to stay home with my younger brother, so Mother decided that Cory, my brother a year younger than me, and I could stay home with Joey while she attended to the business that had to be done. So we sat on the floor, watching the black-and-white TV. Some people had colored paper put over the face of the TV to make the picture seem to be in color. We didn't have that. We only had one TV, sitting in the living room, which was a somewhat large room with painted white walls that were marked up with drawings that we children did when Mother wasn't looking. She tried to wash the walls at least once a week to try to keep them clean. But this particular day was a Tuesday, and Mother usually washed walls on Saturdays.

Anyway, there we were, sitting on the floor watching the black-and-white TV, when we heard a *knock, knock, knock* at the door. My brothers and I were startled. Who could know that anyone was home at this time? It could not have been Mother, for she had a key. Who could that be? My brothers and I had already made plans—if someone was to break into the house, we would get the kitchen knives and fight them off. So the three of us got up, wide eyed and puzzled, and went to the door, and me being the oldest of the three, I got to the door first, putting them behind me and looking at them with my index finger to my lips. In a very soft voice, I said, "Shhhhhh." I then used my adult voice, mustered up some courage, and said, "Who is it?" My brothers were crouched and ready to run and get the knives at my command, if we needed them.

"It's George," came the reply. We were so relieved. It was our uncle. So we opened the door and let him in. It was good to have an adult in the house. After locking the door behind him, we went back to our spots on the lanolin floor in front of the TV. Mother didn't allow us children to sit on the furniture in the living room, because we were always bouncing around and tearing stuff up. But we didn't mind. We liked watching TV on the floor. So there we were watching the television program *Bewitched* and laughing as Samantha twitched her nose and did her thing, to make magic—*poof*, the whole house was clean without her lifting a finger. Uncle George was sitting on a chair and watching and laughing at the program too, or so we thought. Then he spoke and said, "Hey, do y'all children want some popcorn?"

"Yeah," we replied.

"Here is some money," he said. "Why don't you boys go and get the popcorn and we'll wait here, okay?"

We didn't think much about this. We were happy to be getting popcorn. So the boys left. I continued to sit on the floor watching the TV. I was laughing and enjoying *Bewitched* until Uncle said, "Niece, come here." So being an obedient child, I got up from the floor and came near to Uncle.

I said, "Yes?" thinking perhaps he wanted a glass of water or something. Adults always made us children go get them a glass of cold water.

"Give me a kiss," he said. My little mind thought to itself, *Huh.* Something didn't sit right, but in those days we children were obedient to our elders, so I walked over and tried to plant a kiss on his jaw, but he turned and planted a kiss on my mouth. I was so shocked. So I hurried back to my place on the floor and continued watching *Bewitched.* After a few seconds, Uncle called me again. "Niece, come and give me another kiss." Now I was afraid. I didn't know what to do. So I got up from the floor hesitantly, and I could feel his eyes staring at me as I got up and walked over toward him. Each step I took toward him seemed to weigh a ton. I could feel his eyes on me as I looked down and walked forward.

Then *knock, knock, knock* at the door. My heart leaped as I literally ran to the door. It was my two brothers. They were back with the popcorn. They plopped down on the floor in front of the TV, eating popcorn and laughing at the show. I sat down between them. I could not eat the popcorn. My mind could not conceive what had just happened. My brothers gladly ate up all the popcorn. Then Uncle called out, "Do y'all want more popcorn?"

The boys looked eager and happy and said, "Yeah!" as they nodded their heads at the same time. He insisted again that the boys go and I was to stay with him. And he gave them the money, and they left me sitting on the floor watching the TV program. Now I was no longer laughing. No longer enjoying the program. As a matter of fact, I was scared, as you can probably guess by now. He called, "Niece, come here." I was thinking, *Oh my, oh my, oh my.* But I got up as I was told and seemed to be frozen until he said, "Come here." It was more like a command this time. So I went near. "Give me a kiss," he said, so I tried again to kiss his jaw, but again he turned and stuck his nasty large sloppy, wet tongue into my mouth. Now I was crying and so, so afraid. Then he blurted out, "Pull your pants down." So here I was, afraid. Crying and moving back slowly, I pulled my pants down. Then he said loudly, "Your panties too, pull them down." So here I was, so afraid, pulling down my pants, my panties, crying to no avail.

Then *knock, knock, knock.* I hurriedly pulled my clothes up, wiped my tears, and ran to the door. I let my brothers in and this time took them straight to the back room and said to them, "Listen, I don't care what he offers you. You all better say no. No popcorn, no money, no candy—nothing. You hear me?" They looked at me with big wide eyes. They must have seen the fear in my eyes. I said again, almost screaming, "Do you hear me? I mean nothing. You will not leave this house again. We will all stay together."

They nodded as they said, "Yes. We hear you. Nothing. We stay together." So we went back to the floor and watched TV as they ate the popcorn. When they finished, Uncle called out, "Do y'all want more popcorn?"

The boys answered, "No. We okay."

Then Uncle said, "How about some candy?"

The boys said, "No. We don't want none."

So we continued to sit together on the floor. The boys watched TV. Uncle saw that the boys were not going to leave again, so he finally left. When mother came home, I tried telling her what had happened. She said, "Shut up, you just fast, go sit your fast tail down." (This is an afterthought about Mother's statement. I wonder to this day, did she mean tail or tale? Mother used this expression often. As far as I am concerned, she could have meant either. Since she thought I was telling a tale. Or did she think I had a tail? Anyway, back to the situation at hand.)

What? Really? Fast? What is that supposed to mean at the age of eleven? Okay, from that day forward, I was called "fast and stanking" by my aunts, especially the aunt whose husband had molested me. And also by my mother. So I became what she wanted to believe I was. Instead of believing what my uncle had done to me, she chose to believe a lie over what had actually happened. Could it have been that she didn't want to deal or have to confront the ugly things in life? Just wanted to pretend things were all right when in actuality they weren't.

Poem: What's Going on in the World Today?

This old world is not what it seems.
Everyone is trying to achieve some dream.
Everything we see isn't for real.
It'll all pass away, so what's the big deal?
Only what we've done for Christ will last.
Time will stand still, and we'll face our past.
What a blessed day for some it'll be, but
others will cry and gnash their teeth,
as they stand at the judgment seat.
Will their blood be required at our hand?
Or will we proclaim the Gospel while we're still in this land
and there is still time,
for it's not too late, while it's still today,
but the night is coming,
and death will obey.
The dead in Christ will first arise.
Then we who are alive, caught up in the sky.
Jesus, our savior,
will change us all.
Simply because we've lived
and answered His call!
Come. Now. Sinner,
what's really going on?
Except Jesus Christ, God's only Son.
Come to Jesus, who still loves you,
while salvation brings freedom and it's yours to choose.
You've heard about His death on Calvary's cross.
You've heard about His blood shed for the lost.
You've heard on the third day He rose again,
showed His authority over death and sin.
And now hear this once and again
and know for sure, that life doesn't end.
Jesus alone is going on,
because He is God, the loving Son!

Chapter 3
Wait, Then Strike

*Tic...tic...tic...tic...tic...*I was a walking time bomb ready to explode at any given moment...*Tic...tic...tic...tic...toc...tic...*

I remember the time I wanted to kill my supervisor. I had to be about twenty-six years old.

I didn't like this supervisor, and she definitely didn't like me. I had weighed the pros and cons over and over, and I knew that I would end up in jail. So I had to ask myself a couple of questions: Would it be worth it? What about my child? After careful thought, I decided I would go forth with the plan to kill! Now during these times, I cursed like a sailor, and the words I used in this situation were not pretty at all. But I truly hated this woman and wanted to see her demise. So I put my plan in place. A small gun and an opportunity. The gun was easy to get, a small .22. Now I had to wait for the opportunity, and I would put her out of her misery as well as end her harassment. After all, who did she think she was? Ordering us around like we were her slaves on her plantation. Didn't she know these were the '70s? Well, I would show her, or so I thought.

So there we were, at work, and I had to stay later than usual to finish up some papers. I stayed a couple of hours' overtime. Then I bundled myself up to prepare for the cold January weather as I walked to my car. It was so cold that evening, the sun was going down fast, and I pressed my way through the cold. As the freezing winds whipped and bit at the exposed areas of skin on my face, I bent my head down into the warmth of my scarf and placed my hands deep inside my coat pockets, where I could feel the steel of the small gun that I now always carried with me. Carefully, I walked on, avoiding the patches of ice that had frozen from the previous snowfall. As I plowed through the cold night air, I looked up and noticed the shadow of a person in front of me. I focused, squinting my eyes together. I could make out, just a couple of feet ahead of me, a familiar figure. Who could that be? You guessed right. Yeah, my opportunity! I started walking faster. I would catch up with her, and *bang! Bang!*—I would make my kill. Oh yeah, the adrenaline was pumping now. I sped up to catch up with her. She must have felt me 'cause she looked back and recognized me. I could see her face—it looked as if all the blood had drained. It was as white as a sheet, her eyes were large as saucers and frozen with fear, and we locked eyes for just a split second. 'Cause at that moment, she took off running, like a bat out of hell. I had never seen a white woman's eyes so big and afraid in my life. It struck me as sooooo funny, I couldn't even chase her at that point. I was laughing so hard that I had to hold my stomach to keep it from hurting. I saw her jump into her car and start it. She didn't wait for it to warm up or anything. She just sped out of the lot as if the hounds of hell were chasing her. I laughed some more as I got into my car. Then I said to myself, *She is not worth my time, nor me going to jail. All that bad talk she did at work, and now, out here, with just her and me, she runs scared.* I said, *She is nothing but a big fat coward.* As I thought about the scene for a few more minutes while waiting for my car to heat up, I snickered and then drove off into the cold night air.

When I returned to work that Monday, I told everyone what had happened (except the gun, of course), and we all laughed so hard. From that day forward, she never messed with any of us again. After a few months, we never saw her again. Word had gotten around that she had quit or resigned or something. Anyway, *tic…toc…tic… toc…* I was waiting to explode.

Poem: Time-out

No time to sit down, no time to be tired.
No time for shucking, no time for jive.
No time to give up and no time to lie down.
No time for acting out or just messing around.
No time for jesting, no time for lusting.
No time for evildoers. No time for hate pursuers.
No time for backbiting. No time for losing the faith
and not fighting for what's right.
No time to be weary. No time to slack in being serious.
No time for lagging behind.
No time to drag others to the ground.
No time to hold to one's hurts. No time to remember and
harp on past dirt.
No time for hoarding up money. No time for not
trusting.
No time for being funny. No time for being
ashamed.
No time for play. No time for games.
No time for keeping goods in earthly vessels.
No time to be lukewarm, with no heavenly treasures.
No time to boast about what you got.
No time for hurting and cursing others out.
No time for foot stomping. No time for finger popping.
No time for forsaking God's church.
No time to brag about your stuff. Time is winding up.
And
the nighttime will come. When the day is done.
And Jesus will return.
Like a thief in the night, He will appear suddenly.
For some, it will be Joyous. But others will hide
and run with fright.
Nevertheless the time is on us. We must choose right now
what we gonna be about.
For no man knows the time or hour,
but time is running out! No time!

Chapter 4
Soul Mates Are Never Born

What are the signs of a good relationship? I thought I had found my soul mate. At the age of sixteen, I was pregnant and still in school and didn't know much of anything. But there was this one thing I knew: my dad would kill me if he knew that I was pregnant. After all, he had threatened me time and time again. I remember when I was about thirteen, I was trying to see young boys at the house. Of course we had to stay on the porch, but my dad didn't like it at all. Once he had tied my hands together with one of those clothesline ropes and told me he would hang me by my hands in the closet for the whole night if I ever seemed to have any interest to become more than just friends with any of these boys. I remember being so afraid. The thought of hanging in that small dark closet all night long brought tears to my eyes. And he just looked at me and through my tears and what seemed to be down into my soul and said, "Yeah, I'll do it. I'm not playing with you. Do you understand me?"

I nodded between my sobs. "Yes."

Then he untied my hands and said, "Go on, get out of here 'fore I hang you up right now."

I got up and almost ran out of the room, wiping my tears. I went into my room, which I shared with my sister Carmen. Thank God she was in the front room watching TV. I didn't want any of them to see me crying. I sat silently on my bed, sulking and thinking. I was afraid of my father, but it didn't stop me from liking boys and keeping up with the crowds. I just decided to sneak around instead and hoped not to be caught. Maybe if Dad would have been more positive in my life instead of negative, with threats and name-calling, maybe things would have been different. He was always threatening and calling my brothers and me negative names. We rarely received any positive words, encouragement, or reinforcement from him. It wasn't that we didn't believe his threats; we believed the threats, and so we decided to sneak out and do the things we wanted. So threats didn't always help. Where there's a will, we as children would always find a way. When I think back on this, there should have been some balance—or preferably more positive than negative.

Anyway, back to my soul mate. And so there I was, sixteen years old and pregnant. What was I to do? I wasn't going to tell Mother. I had lost all trust in her at the age of eleven. So what was a girl to do? Abortion? Some of my friends had done it, and they were okay. Some had had two to three abortions, and we weren't even seventeen years old yet. But I continued to talk to my friends. They never encouraged me to get an abortion. They just told me their experiences with the abortions. One of my friends said she had done it herself with a coat hanger. Wow. Well, I was too sacred to do that. But I piled up all the information on abortions that I could get from my friends and decided, yes, I would do it. I was already three months pregnant, sick every morning, and having these crazy cravings.

I think Mother missed the pregnancy because I've had stomach problems in the past and had been to see several doctors as a young child. I had nausea and vomiting and couldn't eat a lot, and most food would make me sick. I remember my sister and brothers were glad that I couldn't eat chicken, eggs, and certain meats and vegetables, because that meant more for them. After all, there were eight of us, and Mother struggled to make ends meet. So when I would sit down at the table, my sister would look at my plate and say, "Do you want that chicken?" I would say no. And she would say, "Give it to me," and she would grab the chicken before my brothers. And that had went on well into my teen years. As a matter of fact, it was during this pregnancy that my appetite picked up, and I don't recall having any other problems eating and keeping food down from that time on. Now I ate too much. I sometimes told myself I was making up for lost time. So abortion it was.

I told my soul mate about having an abortion, and he agreed. We decided to tell his mother, and she helped us. I had already called the hospital and had counseling sessions. So his mother and he just went along as my support. And I was glad I was not alone. I felt so empty after the abortion. I cried with my soul mate holding me in his arms. I didn't really understand why I was crying. I just felt kind of cold and empty. But that was done, and the abortion was over. That was the end of that. Or so I thought. But I could never get it out of my head. I would have dreams about that baby over and over again. Even after I had my other children, I would always dream I had another baby somewhere that I could never find. I was haunted by this abortion until I got saved.

Poem: God's Reign

The Lord still reigns in His holy hill.
God of creation. No other still.
What we do for Christ, our Savior,
shows the fruit of our labor.
The fruit is good, or it is bad.
And if I see the fruit you are bearing
as rotten in deed,
why do you say, "Don't judge me."
For when I acknowledge what is displayed,
it's in hopes that you will
someday
demonstrate the love of God,
keep his commands, and obey His Word.
So that life would not blot out
the love that once was in your heart.
For while time is and day remains,
the tree can still make a change, so
be determined. His face you'll seek
until the end of time completes.
Then Christ our Savior will finally come
and receive our labor with good returns.
Now look up and be still
'cause Christ still reigns in His holy hill!

Yeah, and I wound up pregnant again at the age of eighteen, but I wasn't going to have another abortion. I was a senior, about to graduate, and so I married my soul mate right out of high school. But this man was a long way from being what I thought was my soul mate. We argued a lot and had a few fights. The fighting started with my second pregnancy. I couldn't believe this man was fighting with me while I was pregnant. This was our first fight, and I didn't fight back. We were at one of his friends' house. We had a few drinks, and the next thing I knew, this man was up over me, hollering and hitting me across my head. I was so surprised. His friend too. So I just put my hands up over my head and kind of curled up in a ball to try to protect the baby. I couldn't believe this was happening. So from this time forward, this man thought it was okay to disrespect me.

We had another fight about three months later in our own apartment. Again we had been drinking. I was pregnant, and he hauled off and hit me and almost knocked me off the chair. Again I was shocked but not as shocked as before. This time I was trying to fight back, but still the pregnancy made it awkward and difficult, especially since I didn't want to hurt the baby. Of course I went into labor a month earlier than expected and delivered a baby boy. My soul mate was nowhere to be found when I went into labor and when I delivered. But his mother was there and helped me to get to the hospital. And so it was, this man thought that he could disrespect me, and I would just lie down and take it. He should have listened to his mom. When she first met me, I overheard her tell him then, "That girl is ghetto." She had never really approved of her son being with me. Maybe she thought they were better. And maybe they were. They came up on a nicer side of town. His dad (bless his soul—he had passed a little while after we were married) had been a lawyer.

Anyway, the last fight we had, we were married. Our baby boy was about fifteen months old. It was about 2:00 p.m. on a Saturday. He had slept in late after getting off work at 3:00 a.m. We were in the baby's room. I was dressed and sitting on the extra bed and folding the baby's things. The baby was in his little crib, asleep, and my husband was across the room. He had just gotten up and had come into the room to argue. I think he was preparing to go out that night and didn't want me questioning him about anything. He was across the room from me, getting some towels and fussing about the towels, me not cooking, etc. He was still in pajama bottoms. He didn't have a shirt on and started walking toward me. We were pretty heated, and in the midst of me counterattacking his insults, the next thing I knew, he walked over and...*whack*. He slapped me in my face and began to walk away with this smug sort of look on his face.

There was this really long steel pick sitting near me—you know the ones, the kind that we used to pick out our big 'fros. I grabbed that thing, jumped off the bed and onto his back, and started jabbing him with that pick. We were tumbling onto the floor as he hollered from the pain. I kept right on jabbing him with that pick and cursing as we tumbled back and forth. Finally he was able to get loose from me. He jumped up and went into the bathroom, shouting, "I'm bleeding! I'm bleeding! Are you crazy?"

I grabbed my baby and my car keys and headed out of the door. I was tired, tired of the fights, tired of the struggles. I was leaving, but I had to go through his mother's house (who lived downstairs) to get to the garage. Her guests and she were sitting around the table playing cards, laughing and drinking beers. I passed by them quickly, without saying a word, and was out of the door with my baby in my arms and my car keys in hand. I got the baby strapped into the car seat, then noticed I was blocked in by one of the visitors' car, so I went back into the kitchen, where the guests and my mother-in-law were. I could hear my husband fumbling around upstairs. So I quickly spoke to the guests. "Whoever has the red Chevy, could you please move it? I need to get out." I noticed that his mother shook her head at one of the guests, as if to say, "No, don't do it." Then they just looked at me as if I were crazy. Then they acted as if I never said a word. They just kept playing cards and drinking beers and laughing. No one moved from out of their chairs. They were just *sitting*! So I walked back toward the door where the garage was and said, as I was opening the door, "Well, I'll just run that clickety clank… over!" (Now you can fill in the clickety clanks with what makes you feel comfortable, but back in those days before I was saved, my words were not pretty at all.) But boy, you should have seen those people jump up from that table! By the time I had gotten in my car and turned the ignition, *every* car in the drive had been moved. The path was clear. I left that house, that husband, and never looked back, and that was the end of my "soul mate" days.

Poem: Love Lifted Me

Love lifted me up to where the throne room is,
high into the depths of Him
who rescued me from a life of sin,
from guilt that burrowed deep within.
This enemy, my foe, became my friend.
Bought with it pain and shame that staked a place
and shared a space
that populated my mind with mere disgrace.
Kept my eyes blinded, my thoughts captivated.
My ears dull of hearing, my heart desecrated.
My soul lost. My spirit unfree.
Until love stopped by and lifted me.
Love lifted me up into His marvelous grace.
Put joy in my heart. Put a smile on my face.
Opened my eyes, so I peered into His wonderful Word.
I gazed into His powerful plan.
I saw the wonders of His love.
I saw the purpose of His Lamb.
As I tasted, I saw that God is good.
As I feasted, my life once dead now flourished.
As He increased, the weights decreased.
The chains were loosed; old habits fell.
Sin lost its grip; guilt lost its spell.
The love that was out was now within,
and it didn't have to wrestle
long with sin.
Since God Almighty now resides within,
the devil knows he cannot win.
With grace and mercy as my friends,
the guilt and pain has now all ceased.
I've been freed from iniquity.
That's when I realized again
that love lifted me!

Chapter 5
Relations and Relationships

So guess what? Here I was back to where I started from, living with my mother and father. After all, how bad could it be? I was now a grown-up, and surely I wasn't gonna be intimidated by my dad. And so I lived with my parents for about nine to twelve months, and in this process I met my new friend, Wayne White. We were seeing each other on a regular basis and enjoyed one another's company, but it wasn't long after our relationship began that my father started complaining and harassing me, telling me what I could and could not do in his house, telling me he expected for me to be in the house by 10:00 p.m., what ladies do and don't do, etc. Really? I was twenty years old, had a baby and a job, and was separated from my husband. What was he talking about? Was he crazy? These were the kind of thoughts that went through my mind as he complained.

And so I moved out with my son and into a place with my new friend. We got along okay. He also had a son who was about one year older than mine, and so the four of us lived together and did pretty well. After about eight years into this relationship, I became pregnant. The thought horrified me. It brought back memories of my relationship with my husband, and I wanted no more of that. When Wayne found out that I was pregnant, he asked me to marry him. But I wanted nothing to do with marriage, and as a matter of fact I told him I was not going to have this baby. He looked shocked and somewhat disappointed. But I didn't care. I just didn't want to end up in the same situation as before, and I thought having this baby would take me there. So I made plans and arranged to have an abortion. When I told Wayne of my plans, he seemed shocked and hurt, all at the same time, and said, "What? You don't have to do this. I will marry you (for the second time), and things will work out."

I replied, "No, for the second time, I don't want to get married, and I don't want to have any more children." I was set, and my mind was made up. The date was set for the abortion, and I didn't care if he wanted to go with me or not, but I was having this abortion, or so I thought.

In actuality, I wanted to be free to walk away anytime I thought that things weren't going in the manner I wanted them to go. I didn't want to have to fend for another child by myself. And so my plan was set, and I was ready to go forth with it. So later around the time when my appointment for the abortion was near, Wayne handed me a small pamphlet. "Here," he said. "Could you please read this before you continue with your plans for an abortion."

As I took the pamphlet from his hand, I said, "Okay." I thought to myself, *Sure I'll read it, but it's not going to change things. I'm still having this abortion.*

So I went into our bedroom, sat down on the bed, opened the pamphlet, and began to read. After I read and closed the pamphlet, the words rehearsed over and over in my mind, about how they would use a vacuum to suck the baby from the womb and how the baby would be ripped apart piece by piece, one part at a time. I thought about the poor, innocent little baby that was in my stomach being ripped apart. I thought about the pain that the child would experience and sat on my bed, feeling so sad, with tears in my eyes and rolling down my cheeks...I looked up through my tears and noticed that Wayne had come into the room. He placed a hand on my shoulder and said, "Are you okay?"

I looked up into his eyes, which also looked sad, and said, "How can I have this baby? I don't want to go through the stuff that I went through in my marriage, and how can I have an abortion after reading and knowing what I will be putting this poor baby through? I don't know what I am going to do. If you and I were to break up, then I will have another child to raise on my own, and I don't think that I can do it."

Then he took both of my hands into his, got down on his knees in front of me, and looked into my eyes and said, "You don't have to do this, I'll be with you, and I will help you. I love you. Even if you don't want to get married, I'll stick with you. You will not be alone." Then he put his arms around me and held me tight in his arms as I sobbed and boohooed all over his shirt.

For the first time I felt safe and loved by a man who loved me for who I was, and so after I had finished crying and snotting and boohooing, I agreed to have the baby and to cancel the abortion. So now we were both smiling and feeling good, since we knew the baby would be safe. And since I was going to carry this pregnancy to full term, I went over to my dresser draw and pulled out some bottles that held my stash of black mollies and red devils (I took these to party at night and get up in the morning and go to work—the red devils let me stay awake, and the black mollies allowed me to come down from my high and sleep). Yeah, this was the life that I was living, and these pills helped me to function between being a party girl and a working mom. So I gathered my stash and went into the bathroom. I opened the bottles and poured all the pills down into the toilet and flushed. Down they went as I looked up and into Wayne's face and said, "Well, if we are going to have this baby, I can't continue on this stuff."

We held each other tight and just rocked back and forth, as we comforted each other, and of course he kept his word. After our baby was born, Wayne asked me again (for the third time) to marry him. Again (for the third time), I replied, "No, I do not want to get married."

He said, "This is the last time I'm gonna ask you to marry me."

I said, "Okay, and this is the last time that I will say no."

Poem: Wisdom and Folly

Hey, you, here I am, way up here is where I stand.
Come on up, it's high, where God's commands and statures are.
This is the high road.
It's life in here.
Reach up, take hold, grab on for fear
of falling into
the depths of despair,
for I know you don't want any part of that snare.
That's a trap...Once entangled,
you are bound within the clutches of death and destruction, my friend,
without God, without hope, only a shallow life of sin.

Folly! Folly is my name!
Getting lives and stealing souls is my game.
Hey, you! Hey, you! Here I am.
On the stoop of my doorway are fortune and fame,
and partying's here.
Come on in, come on in, don't you fear.
I've got the goods. Living the life is here!
I won't hurt, I won't bite.
Just come on into my kind of life,
of plush and comfort and all these things,
where you can have pleasures and all your sins.
Just close your eyes, and come on in!
I'll have you feeling good at times,
have you looking at the here and now.
I've got what you want—power, prestige—
And I've got what you don't ... want ... to know...
the lost, the darkness ... in your soul,
your mind, your body, the very essence of your core.
I've got drugs, money, even the ho, ho, whore!
Young men, simple, who can't understand,
I've got something to blow your mind. Come on in,
don't listen to Wisdom, my friend!

Shut her out, shut out her cry,
shut out her plea for your life.
I've got exactly what you need—
no frets, no worries, be my guest PLEASE!

Don't listen to Folly. Choose the straight and narrow way,
for eternal life is its pay.
Sin will bring pleasure for a season, my friend,
but havoc and destruction is at its end.
Don't be fooled by its worldly lures.
Don't be caught by its binding chains.
Once it grips upon your heart,
the love of God gets blotted out.
Wisdom gives an abundance of love.
Slow down, take time, and learn of me.
Run with patience, run to win.
I am Wisdom, crying in the way,
hoping to be a part of your fate.
Come and partake of this, I plead.
And when you've found God, then you've found me!

Chapter 6
Salvation Is Free

And so it was, Wayne and I lived together for years and did pretty good, until one day we went to visit one of his sisters. When we got there, who should we see but Harry, standing in the middle of the front room floor, preaching about salvation through Jesus Christ. *The nerve, Harry of all people, talking about God*, I thought to myself. How dare he preach about God as though he was some God-fearing person. After all, we all knew—and he made it no secret to anyone—that he was a homosexual. Not only that, but he also did drugs, drank booze, partied harder than anyone I knew, would fight in a heartbeat, cut you up if he had to, and cursed you out like no one can. That was Harry, and now here he was, standing in the middle of the floor, telling all of us that stood around about Jesus and salvation. Okay, I did most of the same things that he did, but I wasn't pretending to be some God-fearing person who was trying to tell someone else about God. And at least I knew I wasn't right. But when I think about it, how did I know this? I never went to church. No one in Mother's house went to church. I must have known this from them (my family), defining me for years with all the negative name-calling, and thus I became what was exclaimed.

Anyway, here was this young man (in my mind, *This boy*), preaching about Jesus Christ and telling us that we needed to be saved from our sins. Oh yeah, hadn't I just spoken with Evasta this past Friday at work? I had asked her ('cause everybody knew she went to church and read the Bible every day—why she even read during her breaks and lunch periods, and we all saw her). So on this particular day, I walked up to her and asked, "What do I have to do to become religious?"

And she replied, "Go home and read the book of Saint John." I didn't know much about the Bible, but I did have one at home. I opened it and began reading the book of James, 'cause I couldn't remember what book she had told me to read. I only remembered that the book had begun with a *J*, and so I read the entire book of James. And so now here I was, in my sister-in-law's house, and my mind was working and remembering what I had read as Harry continued to preach at us (at least that's the way I felt about it). The book had said something about cursing and blessing should not come out of the same mouth as bitter and sweet waters do not come out of the same fountain. So these words were a conviction to me because I cursed like a sailor, but now I could use them on Harry because I knew that he, too, cursed a lot. So here was my moment of glory, to use these same words that convicted me to make him feel guilty too. My mind went to work.

"Okay, Mr. Harry, I've got something for you." With my hands on my hips, I blurted out, in a matter-of-fact tone, those words that I remembered from what I had read. "Harry, how dare you preach to us. The Bible says that cursing and blessing don't come out of the same mouth. Bitter and sweet waters don't come out of the same fountain." Then I thought to myself, with pride, *I've got him now. I'll shut him down, the nerve of him...*

I think in some strange way, I thought that I was defending God against people like us. But Harry took me by surprise, and my thoughts were cut off as he came back with, "You are right, this is so true, and I am so glad that God has saved and delivered me from all the cursing, the homosexuality, the drugs, the alcohol, the prostitution—girl, you don't know how glad I am. I now know that God didn't make Adam and Steve, but Adam and Eve." He went on to say, "I've given up all these things because God has saved me, and I am ready to live the rest of my life loving and serving God."

He seemed so full of joy as he spoke, but I still didn't want to believe him and said, "Get out of here, I don't believe you." I put my hands on my hips and shook my head from side to side to say, "No way would God save you."

Wayne's sister, who also didn't believe in God, stepped forward, placed her hand on Harry's shoulder, and said, "Listen, I don't know about all this God stuff, but I do know this boy. And for the past couple of weeks, this is all he has been talking about. I saw him flush down the drugs and pour out bottles of alcohol. He's no longer partying, and when men call him, I have heard him say to them that he is saved and they need to be saved. He tells them about God making Adam and Eve and not Adam and Steve. This boy has really changed. I can hardly believe it myself."

So, as I looked from him to her and back at him, I believed. I knew my sister-in-law would never make up anything about this subject. As a matter of fact, she was a person who just spoke her mind, and she didn't care if you were hurt by what she said or not. And when she spoke, it was the truth no matter how harsh it might have sounded. That was the type of person she was. As I thought on these things, I decided I wanted in, and I wanted it bad. I was tired of my life the way it was. I wanted God. And so I asked, "If God did all this for you, then what can He do for me?" That was all I needed to ask, and from that question, my whole life changed.

Harry said, "I am glad you asked that question." He went on to say, "Jesus died for your sins too. He wants you to acknowledge your sins to Him and ask for forgiveness, and ask Him into your life, and He will deliver you, girl. Jesus will save you too!"

I stood there listening and hearing for the first time the plan of salvation and said, "For real, will He really save me?"

Harry looked at me with concern and care in his eyes and said, "Yes, yes, He will save you too."

I said, "Is that all I have to do?"

He said, "Yes, that's all."

I thought about Arriana at work, who was in the Jehovah's Witnesses faith. When I asked her about me getting religion, she gave a list of things that I had to do before I could become religious. She said I had to stop drinking, stop cursing, stop partying, stop wearing short dresses, stop smoking, stop hanging with hoodlums, and so on. I remember it like yesterday because I threw my hands up in the air and said, "There must be no hope for me, 'cause I can't stop all of these things." I remember walking away, with my head down, feeling sad and doomed for eternity. And as I walked away from her, I remember saying to God, *Well, Lord, I guess I'm going to hell.* From that day on, I had never again inquired about religion until this past Friday evening at work, when I got up my courage and asked Evasta. But now here was this boy, telling me salvation is free through Jesus Christ and I could be saved by asking for forgiveness of my sins and believing Jesus died and rose again to pardon or forgive me. So this time, I left the room with hope instead of doom, my heart pounding with excitement as I rehearsed the words over and over again in my mind.

As I went about the rest of the day, I tried to shake off what Harry had told me about salvation, but I couldn't. *Can God really save me?* was the question that stayed on my mind. *I don't know,* was the answer that kept coming up. But that night, I tried to get down on my knees and pray to this God. Wayne was watching TV as I kneeled down at the other end of our bed to pray. As I meditated on what to say, I heard a voice that mockingly said to me, *Get up off your knees, you fool, praying to some God.* So I immediately got up. I was shocked. I looked around the room. There was no one except Wayne, who was still watching TV as if he was oblivious to all that had went on. I went into the kitchen, got a glass of water and then came back into the room, got into my bed, and laid down to go to sleep, but I couldn't. I continued to think about all that Harry had shared about salvation and Jesus forgiving my sins. So I laid quietly in my bed, with my eyes closed, and began to pray, *Okay, Lord, I know I am sinner. No one had to tell me that much. As a matter of fact, Lord, I've done so many sins that I am ashamed to even speak of them, but since You are God, I know that you already know all of them, and I am asking You to forgive me and please come into my life. I am tired of living the way I live. I need you and want you.*

Then all of a sudden I felt as though I was being lifted from off the bed and being rocked back and forth. I felt like everything evil was leaving my body. Then there was a peace, and during this peaceful moment, I felt as if I was being constantly rocked back and forth, being soothed. As I continued to enjoy this moment, after some seconds, which could have been minutes (I'm not sure), a voice spoke to me and said, *Now stop this fornication.* I immediately opened my eyes and looked around the room. There was no one but Wayne, still in the same spot, watching TV as if he heard or saw nothing. I said in an excited voice, "Wayne, Wayne, did you hear that?"

He said, "Hear what?"

I said, "That voice. It said to stop fornication."

He said, "What voice? And stop what?"

I said, "Fornication."

He said, "What's that?"

I said, "I don't know, but I'm gonna find out. Let's call my aunt. She goes to church. She'll know what it is."

And so we called my aunt, and she explained to us what fornication was. And I knew from that conversation that I had to get married or separated from Wayne. We could no longer live together in an intimate relationship. So I prayed, this time with ease, *Lord, okay, I am going to stop this fornication. Wayne has asked me to marry him three times, and I think it would be wrong to just leave him. If it is okay with you, I will marry him. I will know it is okay if you give him a job. If not, then I will leave him.* And wouldn't you know, the very next day, the telephone rang. It was Wayne's old job.

"Mr White, would you like your old job back. We are in need of someone, and if you like, the job can be yours." Wayne accepted with joy. Wayne had been off work for some time now. We had been living off of my income and some aid money that he was able to receive after his unemployment money had run out. And so Wayne and I were married in that same year, and Wayne has never been out of work since, except the time he had to have surgery and it took longer than he had expected to heal. During this process, he lost his position from his current job and would have had to reapply except God intervened again.

Poem: A Testimony

This is the story about
a husband and wife who were married,
not a few years, but a lot.
Most people would say to them, "Thirty-six years."
Then what you get is what you got.
But the gist of this story is
the wife was saved and the husband
was not.

The husband had an affair, and the couple separated
for more than a year.
They came back together, not at God's direction,
but because the husband promised
that he had changed. And the wife wanted
to believe the same.

The husband tried to be true to his promise.
He tried to do the right thing.
But evil was ever present with him because
he had not surrendered his life to God,
so his heart could not be changed.

Even in this, the favor of God was with him—why?
Because he, too, deserves a chance.
What God does for one, he does for the other,
because God is fair, and he still works,
even in the midst of our mess.

So this husband continued to gamble and
do his ungodly things, but the wife purposed to
trust in God, who awarded her grace
to endure this hurt and shame.

And there were other things that
the husband brought in
that could have caused fighting,
cursing, divorce, and separation.
But God granted this wife peace
in the midst of a bad and difficult situation.

The man would have lost the very house
they lived in, but God's favor stepped in.
When the wife wasn't even supposed to have known,
God made it known to her, and she made plans
with the mortgage holders
and kept the house out of foreclosure.

This was well and good for a while,
but after things were all straightened out,
the husband took over the house payments again
and did very well for a while.
When he was injured and needed surgery,
this made him have to go into
a short-term disability bout.
And during the process, it took longer
to heal than expected,
and the disability plan ran out.

He had no money coming into the house.
The wife took over the bills,
and that's when she learned for the second time
that the mortgage on the house was behind.
And for the second time,
the house was about to go into foreclosure.
When she confronted the husband,
he insisted the bills were all paid up
and that things had to have been mistaken
and were not quite as bad as they looked.

Now don't be too hard on the man.
Remember he is a sinner and is doing what he knows.
He doesn't know the good.
He knows what he's used to, a viscous cycle,
something he is unable to get out of.
Now of course the wife didn't understand this,
but God does and did understand,
and his favor was still on the husband and the wife.
Because what God joins together, let no man put asunder.
For God is still in this plan.

Don't be quick to call the wife a fool,
because she had been praying and
seeking God's face through all of this, oh yeah—
She wanted to leave that man.
Many times, she wanted to run away from it all,
but God said, "Not so, but stand and love that man."
How many of you know, that when you run from one thing,
you run into others that are similar or sometimes worse.

Running is not the answer, but stand on the Word of God
and fight, not with carnal weapons of the world,
but know who you really are
and whom you're fighting, and when you've done all to stand, stand
        in the power of God
and be strong in his might and hand.

Well, the woman again made
plans with the mortgage holders
and was able to keep the house out of foreclosure.
And bills were paid on time. In the midst of all this,
she found out
that the husband had spent his 401(k)
and his retirement plan.
He had used up all the funds, and where the money went,
only he and God know,
for he surely didn't tell the wife.

During this period, the husband had
no income, and on top of that
he lost his position at work
(a certified letter was sent to the house,
stating that he would have to reapply
for his position if it became available;
he then could return to the job).
His medical insurance was stopped, and he could
no longer afford to continue the rehab services
that he needed.

So here they were again, the couple, in what
seemed impossible to them,
in what appeared to be a lose-lose situation,
but the favor of God kept them together,
to work through even this.

How many know that it appeared that the wife
was getting the short end of the stick,
but in actuality, she got what she deserved,
for she had also sinned and come short
of the glory of God.
For it was His grace and mercy
that kept her in His love and
from the hell that she, too, knew
she also deserved,
just as it was keeping the husband, and
God made this known to the woman,
every time she wanted to desert him.

Anyway, as she continued, she prayed and
sought God's face, and
God came to her rescue. Money was placed in her hands.
Checks came in the mail
from sources throughout the land.
Every bill was paid, and the doctors

gave favor to the man.
They allowed him visits without payment.

And the $10 gym afforded the rehab services
needed to put him in shape again.
The wife coordinated the exercises,
and eventually his strength returned, and hallelujah!
The job called the house and told the man
if he could return within two weeks,
his position would be held for him.
And hallelujah! Wouldn't you know, it is just like God
to strengthen him right on time.
And the man was back at work again
and given another chance
at life, for in life we are meant to win!

Chapter 7
A New Start

So now what? At the age of twenty-nine, I gave up my life. I surrendered to the Lord. I wanted to allow God to use me in the way that He thought was best. And what a journey it was. I decided to leave school for a while so that I could spend more time reading and studying the Bible, which had seemed to come alive to me. There were so many discoveries, so much I had never seen or even imagined. And I wanted to learn all that I could. School required a lot of my time and became a distraction, so I sat out for a year and used that time to get to know God and His plans for my life.

During this quest, I took off all of my makeup and jewelry. I even started wearing dresses instead of pants—well, that wasn't really part of my quest. I had met Allen, whom I was witnessing to on my job. He asked a question: "How are you gonna be saved and wearing those pants?"

"Huh? What?" I replied.

"Yeah," he said, "you can't be saved with those pants on [my first time hearing this]."

So I responded, "So...it's the pants that will keep you from hearing about God and His plan of salvation through Jesus Christ?"

He looked a little puzzled (I don't think he expected that response from me), so he replied, somewhat bewildered and excited at the same time, "Yeah. I was brought up in the church, and women who are saved don't wear pants."

Now I could have argued with him. We could have gone back and forth on some scriptures that would support what I had read and some that would support what he had read, but I chose not to and gave up the pants instead. When I got home from work, I looked into my closet for some dresses and skirts. I couldn't even find one. Now that's just how long I had been wearing pants. I decided to pray about this situation, so I kneeled beside my bed and prayed, *Okay, Lord, if pants are going to be a hindrance in preaching the good news of your Word, then I need some dresses and skirts.* When I had finished praying, I went around my house, completing some things that needed to be done. When I got a chance to sit down, I felt like I needed to look a little closer through my wardrobe. So I got up and went to the closet and began looking through each pair of clothing item, and near the very back, I found some dresses and skirts that were neatly pressed and on hangers—some things that I hadn't worn for years. So I removed them from the back to the front of the closet and started wearing dresses and skirts from that day forward. And so began my days of witnessing to Allen at work. And yes, he listened, as I talked over and over, day after day, about Jesus and God's love for us.

The people on our job were amazed as I witnessed about Christ. They knew me before I had surrendered my life to God and still could not believe that God had really changed me. And so they had all kinds of challenges and questions that they threw at me day in and day out. I didn't mind though. It was hard for them to accept this same girl, and I understood this, and I could feel where they were at, 'cause they knew and had seen me in action numerous times. I used to curse like a sailor, party every night, talk trash, drink whiskey and vodka, smoke drugs and cigarettes, pop pills, gamble, play cards, fight at the drop of a hat, and not be afraid to do anything else that I thought I was big and bad enough to do. "Had she really changed?" became the question of the day. Of course I had to be tested. And why not by my own friends?

Georgette and I were card partners at work. We had become close friends over the years, and we played cards well together. Our friendship was enhanced after our confrontation with some lesbians (in my days before I was saved) from the bowling league that we were on after work hours. On this one particular day, while we were bowling, two women walked up and tried to come on to us. I set them straight right away by saying, "Listen, no offense, but I don't roll like that." But Georgette was afraid. I could see the fear in her eyes, and they were messing with her even more so. She was this blonde-haired, blue-eyed white girl, and she was turning red in the face as they teased and picked at her, using vulgar words and telling her what they would like to do to her. I tried to tell her to ignore them, but she couldn't. After a while, they left and went to the lanes that they were bowling on.

Georgette said, "I am going to the washroom. I'll be back." I then noticed that she had been gone for a while and that one of the ladies who had been harassing her was also not on her lane, so I decided to go and make sure Georgette was okay. I went into the bathroom, and guess what I found.

Yeah, that lesbian girl had my friend hemmed in a corner, saying freaky things to her, and Georgette was shaking like a leaf. She was so scared and red as beet. I looked at her, and she looked at me. Her eyes were as big as saucers. So I walked over to where they were and grabbed the girl by the arm and pulled her off of my friend. She turned around and was now facing me. I looked dead into her eyes and said, "You better leave my girl alone."

Then she squinted her eyes and stared deep into mine and said, "What's this white girl got to do with you?"

I said, "She's my ace boon coon, that's what she is to me, and you had better leave her alone. I know you don't want to tangle with me. I'm from 4-Tray [this was some language we used back in the day to let people know that we had a reputation by association, and we didn't mind fighting and killing], and I've got something for you and yo' girls." That remark made her move back, backing out of the bathroom with her eyes fixed on me, not liking what I said or did, but at the same time not quite sure if she wanted to take a chance. I continued to stare at her until she left the washroom. I wasn't sure what I would be up against from that time forward, but I knew I wasn't gonna be bullied, and I wasn't gonna allow anyone to bully my friend.

Georgette and I left that washroom, and from that day forward, we never had any other confrontation with those girls. And from that day forward, Georgette and I became the best of friends. Now mind you, Georgette is no chicken. She knew how to take care of herself for the most part, and she is taller and bigger than me, and on many occasions after that incident, she had covered my back.

So back at the job, my girl, along with the others, was putting me to the test, to see if I was really saved. "Hey, Mil, you keep on talking about you are saved and all. Is that really real?" Georgette asked with this kind of silly-looking grin on her face.

"Yeah, girl, God has changed me. I am for real."

Now all the others were looking at me as we spoke. They were up to something. Georgette then said, "If you are really saved, why don't you go into that room where those saints are at? I dare you to go in there. Go on. Go in there if you are so saved."

I looked at all of them. They were nodding their heads as if to say, "Yeah." And they, too, said, "Go on. Go in there if you are so saved."

"Who? What room? What saints? What do they do in the room?" I asked. I had questions. I didn't know about any saints in a room, and I wanted to know more.

"You know, that room," she said, "the one over there by the elevators. They go in there every lunch and break. They pray and read the Bible and that kind o' stuff. I've never been in there, but I know they go in and read the Bible and pray. They are the 'for real' saints. I dare you to go in there with them."

"Where is this room?" I asked (loving a challenge and at the same time being curious—prayer, reading the Bible…ummmm, they had my attention).

One of the ladies stood up from the card table that we were sitting around. I stood up with her, and she stepped to the middle of the aisle, pointed her finger, and said, "You go down there and around that corner, and they are in the first room on your right. They are always there."

Now everyone of the card players were looking at me with those funny grins to see what I would do. So I left my friends and headed in the direction stated, until I got to the room on the right. The door was closed, so I knocked. A voice said, "Come on in."

I opened the door and walked in. I said, "Hi, I am Millicent, and my friends tell me that you all read the Bible and pray in this room."

They spoke and introduced themselves to me, then asked me if I would like to join them. From that day forward, I had a new hang-out. I spent my lunch and breaks with the "for real" saints, and what a glorious time we had in that little room as we talked and shared, prayed, and cried together.

Of course, Georgette and the others were shocked. I remember one day as I walked past them, on my way to the prayer room, they were sitting at the card table, and one of them asked me, "Are you gonna play cards with us today?"

I answered, "Naw, I am going to go to the prayer room, but thanks for asking, and thanks for showing me the room."

I heard one of them say as I moved past them, "See there, Georgette, you had to go and open your big mouth. Now we no longer have our card partner."

I heard Georgette just chuckle and say to them and kind of to herself, "And so I did, well, I'll be, whoever would have thought that she was for real?"

Poem: Servants, Stand Up

Servants, get up stand up and look up.
It's time to be about what God wants.

Servants, stand strong,
Shoulder to shoulder, arm to arm.
Be that burning light that will never go out,
even when your soul gets weary,
even when the money gets tight,
even when you go through
the darkest of the darkest midnight.

Servants, stand fast, fast up, and stand.
Stand against corruption, stand against strife.
The weapons that you war with are not carnal at all
but are mighty through God, pulling down
strongholds that will cause you to fall.

Servants, pray up. Prayer's not a pleasure.
Prayer is a must.
One of the weapons given
by God to us.
So that in him, we have our victory.
In him, we have our trust.

Servants, suit up. Suits of humility will cause
you to stand.
And humble yourselves under
God's mighty hand,
'cause the lifting up of self
is the fall of man.
'Cause it's pride, which is like salt
without flavor—useless, good for nothing in this
dark, desperate, and diabolic land.

Didn't God say, be the light of the world?
Be wise as serpents, and
be harmless as doves.

Servants, speak up.
Say what doth say the Lord.
Live off every God-breathed Word.
Be bold as witnesses.
Stand firm in Christ.
Don't be perplexed by what you see.
Call what's not as though they be.

Servants, look up. See God in his might,
seated on his throne.
The entire kingdom is his heavenly home,
and there's a mansion prepared for you,
a place you can call your own,
inherited through Christ.
The one recognized
by the heavenly dove
as the beloved son of God.
He's also known as the Lamb
who takes away the sins of the world.

Servants, get up. Stand to your feet.
Give God the glory; in him you're complete.
With him you'll rule, rest, and reign,
as kings and priests in his heavenly domain.
But for now you are pilgrims here on earth,
put here for such a time as this.
This is your time to love and serve
and see the bigger picture, 'cause it's not just about us.

Servants, arise. Get up and shine.
Serve heartily today
'cause tomorrow's not promised.

And you want to hear him say,
"Well done,
my good and faithful servant.
Your life was well lived and hid by faith
in Christ, my son!"

Servants, wise up. Get wisdom from above.
Learn to love, study, and live out God's Word.
And don't you dare be in love with this world!

1 John 2:15–18 tells us, "Love not the world."

Chapter 8
Souls Are Won

And so my journey with God continues. And while seeking God, I found out more about myself than what I really cared to know. I found out just how awful I could truly be at times. As God showed me more about myself, the things I used to think were cute weren't so cute anymore, and as a matter of fact, they were downright mean and nasty—and sometimes evil. Like the time when I would pick on Joyce Kitts. Joyce was this tall slender light-brown-skinned girl, with very big eyes and long brown hair. We were in the fifth grade and in the same classroom. Joyce was very quiet and didn't bother anyone. When she did speak, her voice was always low and her sentences short as if she didn't really want to say anything in the first place. The other kids in our classroom would pick on Joyce. They would pull her hair and push, shove, and sometimes hit her. They would call her names like Stinky, Skinny Minnie, Bubbled Eyes, etc., but she never said a word back to them, she never tried to hit or fight back, and she never would tell the teacher. When you would look at her, it seemed as if she were trying to shrink herself into a ball and as if she just wanted to disappear, hide, or vanish into thin air. I would say to her, "Girl, you need to stand up for yourself. Learn how to fight back so that they can leave you alone." But she never did. So I decided to teach her my method for fighting back.

So every day after school, I would hit, punch, and slap her and say, "Hit me back." But she never did. My method was to let her get tired of me hitting, punching, and slapping on her until she would strike back. I should have stopped when I saw that this was not working, but I continued in my madness. I then became the bully, and

I was worse than the other children, because I would chase her and harass her after school. It was bad enough the kids in school would push and shove on her, but now she had to endure the harassment outside of school as well. Thanks to me, the girl couldn't get a break. So every day at 3:15 p.m., the school bell would ring, and Joyce would be at the front of the line and the first one out of the building. She would take off running. And boy, could she run. But I would chase her until she was tired and had to stop. By the time I would catch up with her, out of breath (she and I both), I would start striking at her between breaths and say, "Hit me back." She never would.

I continued this madness, day after day, until one day when I had caught up with her, her younger sister was standing with her. Her sister was about a year or two younger than us. She was short and chubby, with light-yellow skin and short curly light-brown hair. Her eyes were as big as her sister's. Cisley (I later learned her name) looked me right in the eyes and hunched up her little shoulders, as if she was trying to gain some more inches to make herself taller. Her two fists were clenched into balls as if she was ready to fight, and she said to me, with a very loud but strong voice (as though she was a linebacker or something), "You better leave my sister alone."

I looked into little Cisley's face. Her cheeks were chubby and red as roses. I stared into her eyes, they were wide and big as saucers, and I said, "Yeah, and just what are you going to do?"

Little Cisley didn't flinch, didn't hesitate, and didn't back down. She just seemed to square her shoulders even more (and it appeared as if she were looking down into my soul), and she said again, "You better leave her alone."

As I looked at her, I had to admire her courage, her nerve, her strength, and her love for her sister, so I said, "Okay." Then I moved out of their path, and they left together. From that day forward, I never bullied Joyce again. As a matter of fact, I never picked on anyone in that way since that day. I don't think I was afraid of her sister. I knew it took a lot of guts to do what she did, and I admired her courage.

And you know, thirty-five years later, I met Joyce again. I was working for Saint Ailbe's Holistic Center, counseling a group, when who would walk in, to describe the available resources, but Joyce Kitts. I recognized her immediately the moment she entered the room. Our eyes met for a brief second because she immediately dropped her gaze to the floor as she moved across the room and took her seat. As she spoke to the group, I tried to make eye contact with her, but she was not having it. I couldn't blame her though. Who would want to acknowledge someone who had been so nasty to them? All the memories from our childhood days flooded my mind as I was sure that those unpleasant memories must have come back to her mind as well. After she finished her session, she did not linger around. She got up from the chair and left the room just as she had come in, looking down, to avoid any eye contact with me. I had to finish up with the group. Then I went into my director's office and asked for the last name and office room number of the resource lady, and she gave me the information.

On my lunch break, I went up to her office, which was on the other side of the big building and on the top floor. When I got to her room number, her name was on the white glassed door. She was the director of Resources. I knocked lightly at the door, and she said, "Come in."

I opened the door and went into the office. I said, "Hello, Joyce, I am Millicent Hinton. Do you remember me?"

She sat at her desk and looked at me from across the room, sitting and looking so comfortable in the beautiful grained leather chair that she sat in. Then she spoke and said, "Yes, I remember you. Come on in and have a seat." So I walked over and sat in one of the two seats that were across from her desk. She said, "What can I help you with?" She was still soft-spoken and very pleasant.

I didn't beat around the bush. I got right to the point and said to her, "I want to apologize for all the wrong I did to you when we were children. I was cruel and mean, and what I did was very wrong. I am very sorry."

Our eyes met. This time she didn't drop her gaze. She looked at me as I looked at her, and she said, "I accept your apology."

I felt somewhat released and told her how relieved and glad I felt. (I knew that she didn't have to accept my apology, and if the shoe had been on the other foot and if I wasn't saved, I know it would have been hard for me to accept the apology of someone who had done me wrong.) So I continued to say, "Thank you, I am grateful to and for you." I said this several times. Then she changed the subject and asked about my family, my life, my career, etc., and we talked as old friends instead of enemies.

When I got up to leave her office, we hugged and parted as friends. Man, what a small world. My lesson is, be careful how you treat others, for you never know what life holds for you in the future.

How can a person be good and yet bad and bad and yet good? My poor husband thought I was gone for sure. He would say things like, "You have done a 360-degree turn on me. I like the made-up you better, with the makeup and jewelry and the way you used to dress." He would also say, "I want the old you, the way you used to be," but I think he was just as confused—or should I say mixed up—as I was. 'Cause he liked the new me as well. (If I was sick and didn't read my Bible, he would say, "Would you like for me to get your Bible for you?" Or if I missed church, he would say, "Why aren't you going to church?"—things like that. He liked the change. He didn't want me to backslide.) I guess this was love.

But love can take you places you don't want to go but at the same time you need to go to. That was what love did in our relationship. So we had all this new stuff going on. I had studied the Bible for over a year, without interruptions from school. I was witnessing to people everywhere I went, with him or without him—on the buses, the streets, the trains, on the job, in the family, it didn't matter. Wherever I went, the Gospel was preached. I spoke about God morning, noon, and night. I ate and drank the Bible. It was my life. There was always so much, and I had to find out more and more. The more I learned, the more I needed to learn. So now here I was, back at school, pursuing my career.

Little did I know that my husband was drifting further and further away from me, until one day the ugly truth hit me square in the face. He was having an affair. Was I shocked? Yeah. And yes, the bickering started. I bickered with him day and night (he called it nagging), but I noticed I was getting nowhere with all the bickering, so I tried talking with him. I asked the question that most people ask when they find out that their spouse is having an affair: "Why?" He had no answers and made no excuses. (After he had gotten past the denial stage, when he could no longer deny, 'cause by this time I had all the proof on paper and sat it down in his face. Man, what a mess. This could be a whole other session, if I went into how I accumulated the facts and how he had still denied.) So I asked, "Do you want a divorce?"

"No," he said.

"Are you willing to stop the affair?" I asked.

"No," he replied.

So by this time I was confused—I mean mixed up—so I said, "Okay, then I would like for you to leave."

"No, I am not leaving. I am staying here," he said.

Now I was mad all over again. "What?" What did he want? So I blurted out in an angry voice, "So what do you want, your cake and cookie too?"

He just sat there on the couch and looked at me with this sort of smug look on his face as if to say, "You got it."

I have not been this mad in a long time. I jumped off that couch and launched at him with clenched fists and arms flailing through the air. I was so furious I wanted to tear him apart, to scratch out his eyes, but he was able to grab both of my arms and hold me in a pinned-down position until I calmed down. After I had calmed down, he let go of me and walked out of the room. After I had settled down and collected my thoughts, being oddly calm, I went into the bedroom where he was and said again, "I need for you to leave."

And his response again was, "No, I am staying."

This kind of thing makes you wonder... *What the what?*

My life seemed to spiral downward from here. I felt myself as though I was crumbling, falling to pieces. What was I going to do? I cried and cried until I couldn't cry any longer. I couldn't eat because the food tasted like cardboard. I could barely talk to anyone, and I had to push myself to stay in school, to study, and to take care of the daily activities that were my responsibilities. I thought to myself, *So this is depression.* For the first time in my life, I was experiencing real depression, but by this time I had enough of God's Word in me to know to call on Him, so I got down on my knees and knelt beside my bed and said, "O God." As the words began to pour out of me, a fresh set of tears started, and I cried and cried. Between sobs I said, "God, O God, why? Why? Why?" Then for some strange reason, I started telling God all the things that I had done for Him (as if He owed me something). "Didn't I go to Michelle's house when you told me to, even when I knew she didn't want to see me?"

See, Michelle and I had been childhood friends, and when we reconnected as adults, I found out that she was now in the Jehovah's Witnesses faith. My brother had run into her a few days before and had given me her telephone number. At that time, I called and got her address. I thought it would be good to see my old friend again. To see how she had fared after all these years. When I made my visit to her house, I found out that she was doing pretty good for herself. So she, her mother, and I sat in the big kitchen area of her house. As we talked and laughed about the good ol' times, they were picking collard greens. It was so good to see them both and to know that they were doing well. Then Michelle asked, "So, Mil, how has life been treating you these days?"

"Very well," I replied. "As a matter of fact, I am even saved."

Both Michelle and her mom looked at me with puzzled expressions on their faces and said, "What do you mean?"

I explained to them how I had allowed God to come into my life and how my life had changed as a result. They looked at each other, smiled, then said, simultaneously, "Oh…we are studying with the Jehovah's Witnesses faith."

So there we were (in my friend's kitchen), I was talking about my relationship with Jesus Christ, and they were talking about their Jehovah's Witnesses faith. After about thirty minutes or so of us going back and forth like this, I stood up and said, "Well, you seem to be set on what you believe, and I know what I believe. It doesn't seem to me that I will be able to change your minds, and it's darn well sure that you are not going to change mine, so it is time for me to leave." As I got my coat off of the back of the chair where I was sitting, I stood up and said, "It was really good to see you both again."

As I started putting my arms into my coat, Michelle asked, "Will you come back again? We could talk some more about the Bible."

"Of course," I replied. Then I added, "I would love talk about the Bible."

And from this, Michelle and I began our quest to search out God's Word through the Bible, for the truth. I would go to her house from work, day after day. All I would do was talk about Jesus Christ and read passages of the Bible about Jesus Christ and salvation. Michelle would read with me and ask question after question after question. I talked and talked and talked and read and read, and Michelle listened. Now on some days, I would come to her house unannounced, because I had heard direction from God to go to Michelle's house, and she would seem unwilling to let me in. She would say something like, "Oh, I have so much to do," or, "Today is not a good day," or, "Oh, I've got to go out in about another hour," etc. Sometimes she just seemed to have an attitude because I rang her bell, but in all that, I was not deterred.

It was if I was on a mission or something, and each time, I would convince her to let me in by saying things like, "Oh, I will not be very long," or, "Could we spend maybe thirty minutes together," or, "I can walk to the store with you."

And so I kept coming, and she kept letting me in, until one day, I rang the doorbell of her house, and she half-opened the door, peeked out through the small opening, and said in a nonchalant voice, "Oh, it's you."

I said, "Are you busy? If not, I'd like to come in for a while."

She continued to look at me, with the door half opened, as if she was trying to size me up or something. Then she opened the door all the way and said, "Okay, come on in, but you can only stay until my Jehovah's Witnesses people come. They should be here in about fifteen to twenty minutes."

I said, "Okay, that's fine."

Then I entered the roomy little hallway that led into the front part of her house, which was the sitting (or living) room, as we call it. Usually we sat and talked in the kitchen area, but this time she said, "Let's sit up here. I want to make sure that I hear the doorbell. I don't want to miss my Jehovah's Witnesses people when they come."

So we sat up front and talked and talked and read about Jesus, the Son of God; the Father God; and the Holy Spirt of God. We were reading John 14:6 about needing Jesus if we want to have eternal life. It seemed as though we had been talking for about two hours and we were finishing up when the telephone rang. Michelle picked up the phone. "Hello? Yeah...yeah...I am here...I was in the front of the house waiting...What?...No...Hold on...Let me make sure." She sat the phone down, looked at me, and said, "Excuse me," went to the front door and out, rang the bell, and came back inside. She asked me, as she sat down to pick the phone up, "Did you hear the bell?"

I said, "Yeah."

She said, "I did too." She picked the phone up and said, "Yeah, the bell is working. Do you want to come back? Well, okay...I'll see you tomorrow...Bye." She hung the phone up with a puzzled look on her face. Then she said to me, "That was my Jehovah's Witnesses people. They said that they were here about forty minutes ago, ringing the bell, knocking on the door, and waiting for me to answer." Then she said, "I didn't hear a thing. Did you?"

I said, "No, I didn't hear it either."

Then she said, "That's so strange. The bell is working. They said that they were ringing the bell and knocking for almost five to ten minutes. And we were right here. Strange we didn't hear them."

I said, "Yeah, that's strange." After that, I realized that it was late and we had been talking for almost two hours. I got up and told Michelle, "Well, it's time for me to leave."

She said, "Okay." And I left.

After that, I didn't hear from Michelle again until a week or so had passed. She called me on the telephone on a Saturday. I said, "Hi, how are you doing," after she told me who she was.

She replied, "I am fine." Then she continued with, "I want to come to church with you this Sunday."

"Okay," I said, "I will pick you up at 8:45 a.m."

"Okay," she said. Then she continued with, "I left the Jehovah's Witnesses faith."

Surprised, I said, "You did? What happened?"

She replied, "They told me not to see you again. They said that you are a devil."

"What?" I said.

She said, "Yeah, and I told them that they must be the ones who are devils because I knew you before and after God had saved you. And I told them that you were definitely from God. I then went on to ask them, where were they when I was hungry and when I needed clothing? They knew my situation but did nothing to help, and I told them of the times that you had helped me out and looked for nothing in return."

And so my dear friend Michelle got saved and went on to become a preacher of the Gospel of Jesus Christ. She is a mighty woman of God, even to this day.

And in the midst of me telling God what I had done for Him, He gave me my answer. "Why not you?" And then He led me to the book of Ecclesiastes chapter 3: "There is a time for everything."

Poem: Need More Time

Christ is the eternal One. He is God, the Beloved Son.
Once dead but now alive, for the purpose of God
is in Him fulfilled. Says, "Listen, child, be still."

It is time to hear His voice, to heed the call and not be lost.
Eternity is a long, long time. Without God, there's no good
in any of us.
Only dogs, whoremongers, sorcerers too,
murderers, idolaters, and what are you?

All kinds of evil works are conceived and displayed.
You think now and say, "That's okay."
But in the end your eyes will open
to an eternal life of pain and suffering.
Now is the time to accept Christ
as Lord and Savior of your life!
Stop playing and wasting all your time.
The end is near and fast approaching.
The night will come, and no more coaxing.

The soul that dies outside of Christ
will not stand in His sight.
Not before the holy God,
not without His sacrifice.
You don't need more time, but you need Christ,
and you need Him, not tomorrow, but right now!

And so I took my children and left my husband. He continued
to pursue his affair, and I continued to witness about God's goodness
in my life.

Now, here I was at work, witnessing to anyone and everyone that
God puts in my way. And at this time, I met Larry. He and I were on
the same softball team after work. I played the third base, and he played
the outfield. We won the first place trophy that year. Larry was going

through a lot of changes with his wife. He and she had separated, and they were in court battling for custody of their three-year-old daughter. I could relate to him because I, too, had a three-year-old daughter. I could only imagine what it would be like if my husband and I were fighting for custody of our child. So I prayed constantly for Larry and listened as he shared with me the progress on the case.

Then one day while we were at work, the news spread like fire. Larry's little girl had been killed the same day he won custody of his child.

What?…I couldn't believe it…What happened? The mother, they were saying, she killed her own daughter…to hurt him. My good friend, who was also a good friend of Larry's, was crying as she nodded her head, affirming that the news was true. "How awful," she was saying as she continued to cry. "The baby was only three years old," she cried. "Larry is all messed up. He called me this morning…I feel so sorry for him." She was going on and on between sobs and tears running down her cheeks. As I looked at her, all I could think about was poor Larry. I couldn't say anything to Sheena and the others as they continued to talk about what had happened. My mind was just crying out, *Oh God, oh God…*

I pulled away from them and went into the ladies' room. I felt the need to pray, and so I went into one of the stalls, lowered my head to my chest, and began to weep and pray, "God, please help my friend. Don't let him bear this burden alone. O God, if there is any way possible, I am willing to share this load, O God, O God…" Then it happened. The weight that came on me was one I'd never experienced before. I cried and cried and cried. I could feel his sorrow, his pain, his depression. I was sharing in his suffering. God gave me some of the load.

When I attended the funeral, everyone was shocked to see how well Larry was holding up. The mother was there, escorted by the police, in handcuffs, hollering and screaming in torment, "My baby, my baby!" It was as if she had come to the realization of the horror that she had committed.

When I walked up front to greet my friend and his family and to offer my condolences, our eyes met and locked. I looked deep into his eyes, and he seemed to be looking deep into mine. There was a connection. God was at work. It was as if He was showing him that I was sharing his load and showing me that my friend knew that I was sharing the load. So we both were able to see God's work, and we both seemed to know right there that things would be okay. So we hugged each other, and there was nothing else to be said. God did it all.

Larry returned to work, and I returned to the race that was set before me—the race to win souls. I continued to witness to everyone about the goodness, love, kindness, and salvation of the Almighty God.

Poem: The Two Made One

We're in this thing for better, for worse,
no longer to see just self as first.

Now, I admit with my own strength, this'll never work,
so I depend on God to help me…to love.

With Him as my Creator, my God, my Friend,
I move, I breathe, and have my being.

Our lives two, can now be one,
like Christ, the church, God's will be done!

We make these promises, and we should—
to see the things as our Savior would…

The impossibilities made possible, because God
can, and does, take our everyday, average, ordinary plans
and make them so much more,
when we've prayed and placed them in His hands.

We're going into this thing called marriage. It's for life…
We're joined together, united in Christ!

We're manifested in truth, perfected in love,
sealed by the power and covered by the blood,
which enables us to do as our Savior does.

Having compassion, for one another,
a minister, a servant, to a sister, to a brother.

We'll make our vows, no longer to live
doing what pleases our selfish wills.

But dare to show this dying world,
that yes, our Savior really lives!

We're transformable, conformable, apparent, and plain.
United, together, we're under His construction,
advice, and plan.

Waiting on others, esteeming them better than us,
praying for them and putting them first!

Speaking the Word in boldness and love,
telling of Christ's death, burial, and resurrection!

Believing that these that confess with the mouth
and believe with the heart
will also become a part in the family of God.

Then they, with us, will go into all the world,
with humble hearts renewed in love!

We'll be wise as serpents, harmless as doves.
We will walk by faith and trust God's Word.

As believers, we represent the church of God.
As couples, an institution,
joined in union, one to the other,
no longer two, but one in number.
Now this is the plan that God has ordained.
Let no man put it asunder!

We're united in Christ, a part of each other,
and in this mystery, we're seated together
in the heavenlies, where the greatest marriage
supper still awaits.

And surely one day, it's gonna take place.
This institution is ordained by God.

A man, a woman, two flesh made one!
Christ, the church, God's will be done!
Amen!
Lord Jesus, come! (Taken from Revelation 22:20, KJ)

Chapter 9
Nothing Is Too Hard for God

Spreading the good news from house to house and from stop to stop, passing out salvation tracts, stopping to talk and pray with people about God and his goodness to the children of men—this was my life. So one day on my way home from work, I got off the bus and started walking the four blocks to my house. I noticed a group of men standing around, and as I walked by, I heard them say, "Hey… hey," so I stop and turn around (there were four of them, talking and passing an alcohol bottle)."

So I said, "Hi, how y'all doing?"

One of them gave the bottle to another man, then stepped forward, away from the others, and moved toward me and said, "I know who you are."

So I said, "Yeah, well, who am I?"

He was a short, medium-built light-brown-complexioned man with gray eyes, a mustache, and curly black hair. His eyes seemed to smile as he spoke and said, "You are a missionary."

I looked at him as I thought about this title for a brief second, and then I said, "Well…yeah…I am on a mission. I do love the Lord, so yeah, I guess I am a missionary of some sort."

He then said, "I know that. I can see it."

At this, the other men lost interest. They turned around, got into their huddle, and started drinking and laughing with each another. They seemed to have forgotten all about Jacob (he introduced himself to me) and me, and as Jacob and I continued our conversation, I soon forgot about them. It was as if Jacob and I were the only two people on the planet as he said, "I need for you to do me a favor."

"What is it?" I asked.

His eyes seemed to stop smiling and became very serious as he said, "Every time you pass by here and see me, can you stop and pull me aside and talk about God to me?"

I did not hesitate. "Sure," I said, "I would love to do that."

And so it was, every day after work, I stopped that way and pulled Jacob aside from his drinking buddies, and we talked about God and the Bible. He had many questions, and God gave me answers. This went on for months, until one evening, I came by that way, Jacob was more intoxicated than usual. I had never, in the time that we had begun our encounters, seen him this drunk. His speech was slurred, and he staggered as he walked with me away from the other guys. But I kept my word, and we talked about the Lord. This day he had no questions. He just listened as I talked and talked. I talked more than usual this time. When I looked around, I noticed that it had gotten dark and the other guys had already left. So I said, "Well, I guess I had better be getting on home."

Jacob looked at me and said, "I will drive you home."

I said, "No, thanks, I can walk. It's not far."

He said, "No, it is dark. I can't have you walking alone like this. Come on, get in." He opened and held the door of his beige Lincoln Town Car for me, which was parked not far from where we were standing. I looked at him. He was so serious about driving me home and appeared so concerned for my safety, so I silently said a quick prayer and got into the car. As I gave him directions to my house, he didn't say a word. He seemed to be concentrating on the road. Surprisingly, he didn't swivel or swerve as he drove. When we got to the front of my house and I began to open the car door, he took my hand, pulled it to his lips, and kissed it and said, "Thank you. I truly thank you for taking time with me."

So I said, "You are so welcome. I enjoy spending time talking about God. You have blessed me in allowing me to share what I love." As I got out of the car, I said, "Good night, and see you soon." After I got out of the car, he waited until I opened the front door to my house, and then he left. I prayed for his safety as he drove away. From that day forward, I never saw Jacob again on that block. I continued to take that street home from work, but he was never there. I continued to look for him, even asking the men about him. But they didn't know where he was. As a matter of fact, they didn't know much of anything about him, except that they drank together.

After a while, I forgot about him, until one day, some months later, on a Saturday afternoon, I was on my way to a funeral and had to pass that way to get to the bus stop. As I passed that way, Jacob came to my mind, and I said, "Lord, I wonder, what ever happened to Jacob?"

When I got to the bus stop and was waiting for the bus, I heard, *Beep, beep, beep, beep*. I looked up, and I saw a beige Town Car with the window down and Jacob looking out and smiling. He shouted, "Ms. Hinton! Hey…where are you going?" I told him where I was headed. He said, "I am going that way. Come on, get in, I'll drop you off." I said okay and got into the big car. He wasn't drunk or high. As a matter of fact, he was smiling and full of joy as he spoke and said, "I am saved now and in a church where people love me and I love them."

"What?" I said. "That is wonderful. I am so happy for you."

We laughed and talked and praised God all the way to my stop. When I got out of his car, my heart was full of joy, as was his. We parted from each other's company but not the presence of God. Jacob and I never saw each other again, but we both knew that God had performed another one of His miracles. There is nothing too hard for God.

And so here I am today, thirty years later (from the day that God saved my life and delivered my soul from death), struggling within and fighting without. New challenges in unfamiliar territory, trying to make good decisions over bad ones. What do I do now? My health is failing, my parents are older and need care, and my siblings are dysfunctional. How did we wind up here? No one prepared me for this——struggling within, fighting without. I've seen a lot—devils, demons, evil, evil spirits, and evildoings. I've also seen good, mercy, grace, compassion, and blessings. I've been talked about, lied to, mistreated, misunderstood, abused, and misused—and all for the sake of the Gospel. And these things have led me to know that life for me has become a choice between good and evil. No middle ground for me. No excuses. No gray areas. Which will I choose each second (not each day, not each month or year)? It is a conscious choice every second for me. I've come to know that people are not my enemies. My enemy is the devil and the demonic forces that will entice me to make evil choices in that split second that I have to choose the good. And I also know that in order to choose the good, I must read and study the Word of God every day (God's Word is alive and active— you can read Hebrews 4:12), and it will combat the lust of my flesh that ever surrounds me, as long as I'm in this body. The Word of God will help me to stay, to prevail, to live for God's will...

Poem: Stay on the Wall

We're battling and fighting a world unseen,
powers and principalities—plotting, planning,
watching, waiting, wanting for us to fall,
but
I say, you say, he says, she says, "Stay, stay,
stay on the wall."

Forces and spirituality, darkness in high places,
come in many forms and shapes
and…too often familiar faces.
Come to conquer, devour, divide
the very elect, the people of God.
But we have a promise—no weapon a-prosper,
so stay…stay…stay on the wall.

People of God, you…in the light,
praying and fighting to do what's right,
staying the course is no small plight.
It takes some struggle and yes, some muscle…
but without God's hand in
the scheme of these things,
all of our efforts would be a loss,
there'd be no cause,
so stay, stay, stay on the wall.

The adversary, the avenger, the foe, he knows…
We're snatching, empowering the sin-sick souls,
making them ready for destiny's call,
as the mystery of God unfolds…
God was manifested in the flesh,
justified in the spirit, seen of angels,
preached unto the Gentiles, believed on in the world,
and received up into glory…
Now, that's the whole salvation story.

Fix your eyes and heed the call,
and
stay, stay, stay on the wall.

We're willing workers, diligent, strong.
This battle's been fixed; we've already won!
Who will go with us into eternity?
What does God have for me?
There's "a people" here in this community...
Someone else has got to be reached.
Recover the sight of the blind,
loose the oppressed from the state of his mind.
Set the captives free, stop the firing darts,
bind them up—those broken hearts—
and preach the good news of the Gospel to all...
and stay, stay, stay on the wall.

Pastors and leaders,
you've been shepherding God's sheep,
in this desolate land,
not looking at the obvious,
but believing God for the saving of man,
snatching the souls from the fire, from fear to honor,
from devastation to proclamation...transformation...
glances...places
that were wasting away.
Now, new life, new beginnings.
Stand vibrant and tall,
walking not in the counsel of the ungodly,
standing not in the way of the sinner,
sitting not in the seat of the scornful,
but delighting in God's law,
stay...stay...stay on the wall.

People of God, you in the light, where's your bread?
Where's your Word that you've been fed?

Line up, move forward, eyes ahead.
The gate is narrow; the way is straight.
Prepare yourself, get ready to fight,
use the weapons that you've been given.
Cast off the weights and sins besetting.
Live off every Word of God,
and
stay…stay…stay on the wall.

This race isn't given to the swift,
and
the battle is not given to the strong,
but to them that endure till the end!
Put on your belt, gird up your loins.
You're given a spirit not of fear
but of power, love, and a sound mind—this battle is real!
We don't retreat.
Though one may fall, it's never defeat.
United we stand; our feet are firm.
We hold up the banner with the leaders in front.
Who's willing to run?
Make an impact?
It's time to take the territory back!
Not reacting to what we see,
but calling what's not as though it be!
'Cause we know, where there's no knowledge,
the people a-perish.
Where there's no life, the blood a-stagger.
Where there's no peace, confusion abides.
Where there's no joy, allusions reside.
Where there's no hope, despair—
ARISE!
You, who are in the light,
be bold, be tenacious, don't turn back!
In God we trust, in Christ we rest.
For the saints, we ask our God to bless.

In prayer, to our knees we fall.
We never give up. We stay…we stay…we stay on the wall!

In conclusion, will I prevail? No, not alone. God lives inside of me, and He always prevails.

So now I know at least three things:

1. My life is hidden in Christ. When I read Galations 2:20 (KJ), I am assured of that, as it says, "It is no longer I who live, but Christ who lives in me; and the life which I now live in the flesh I live by faith in the Son of God, who loved me and gave Himself up for me."
2. I've been bought with a price and sealed by the promise. 1 Corinthians 6:15–20 and Ephesians 1:13 assure me, as these words read,
   "What? Know you not that your body is the temple of the Holy Ghost which is in you, which you have of God, and you are not your own? For you are bought with a price."
   "In Christ you also trusted after you heard the Word of truth, the Gospel of your salvation, in whom also after you believed, you were sealed with that Holy Spirit of promise."
3. Living for God, will I prevail? I will!

Will Make You Do Right

old song,
         ike you do right when you wanna do wrong."
ᴸ⸱   eat and a heart of its own.
And when you think that you've got it all figured out,
and you know exactly what it means,
love doesn't always appear as it seems.

Love reaches high, and love stretches wide,
so the next time you're down, just give love a try,
'cause love hanged on an old rugged cross
to bridge the gap between God and us,
'cause we were separated, alienated from God,
and lost in the Garden when the fruit was eaten.

Man fell, sin raced through the eras
of time,
cursed generation line to line,
'til God came down from heaven above,
wrapped in flesh and presented in love.

As the God of grace, He cleans us up.
As the God of hope, He lives within.
As the God of mercy, He gives us chance,
over and over, again and again.

'Cause God knows that ol' devil, the enemy of our souls,
had us all fenced in,
because we fell and gave in to sin.
But praise be to God, those fences are down,
and we are recovered from the enemy's camp.
Because of the Blood, the Lamb sacrificed,
we are redeemed and given new life.
We have a new start,

a new beginning, and we even have an expected end,
over death, hell, and the grave.
In Christ, we win!
And love makes it happen again and again!

You know the old song,
"Love will make you do right, when
you wanna do wrong."
Love is patient, kind, and strong.
It's not puffed up. It doesn't seek its own.

But helps those who are weak and feel all alone,
Those who are hurting, abused, and afraid to go on!

Love lifts up from the miry clay,
takes the root of sorrows and cast them away.
Love will place your feet on solid ground and
turn your life completely around.

Onto paths of righteousness, where healing for
your soul is found.
Just call out to God, with pure and fervent hearts.
Love will take your troubled minds and ease your
anxious thoughts!

For it's love, and that's why the marriage super of the Lamb a-take place.
It's love, that's why the mystery of God unfolds by faith!
It's love that gives hope, and we can face tomorrow.
It's love that gives strength, and we will stand these tempting hours.
It's love, and we work while time is called today,
for the night will come, and the time will pass away!

So for now, hold on and trust in God,
'cause faith, hope, and love abide,
but the greatest of these is love!

So love on, each other, my sister, my brother,
and hold on and pray and pray and pray on
and watch God's love
make you do right, when you wanna do wrong!

Chapter 10
Poetry by More Than One Poet

1. Shirley Foster
2. Roy Swan
3. LmHt

Sow a Seed

Sow a seed and meet a need,
'cause love, joy, and peace are what this world
is a slackin' and the people are a lackin'.

Sow a seed and meet a need for it's about
loving the Lord your God
with all your substance and all your heart.
Then you'll see
that God will plant you as a tree,
by living waters, pure and free,
with roots that are thick and deep and
leaves that are full and green,
with fruit that's ripe and flourishing!

Then will you understand
that you are more than just a physical being
with worldly lust and earthly flings.
You were created to be better,
to have joy to soar, to walk, to run and not be weary.
The Holy Spirit, He's your guide.

He'll bring peace
when circumstances and things that are not right
will say to you otherwise!

Sow a seed and meet a need.
Long-suffering and gentleness—
these are not popular by far,
but you must allow them anyhow.
And God will cause you to succeed
in every situation that you meet,
whether good or bad.
Long-suffering and gentleness will see you through,
and God will take the worst of any situation
to bring the best out in you!

Didn't He heal the sick and raise the dead?
Didn't He feed five thousand with two fish and five loaves of bread?
Didn't He make the deaf and the mute hear and talk?
Didn't He cure leprosy and make the lame walk?
Didn't He walk on water, call peace in a storm?
So go on, be gentle even though you may suffer long.

'Cause Jesus died on an old rugged cross.
He was buried in a borrowed tomb.
But on the third day and at the appointed hour,
He got up from the grave and He has all power!

So sow a seed and meet a need.
Goodness, faith, meekness increase!
Which cannot be ignored. Given the times of today,
goodness needs to have its way
in us, through Christ, so all can see
His goodness, His glory, His righteousness,
which we receive by faith, in knowing this One that we believe
and working His works 'cause we are free!
For faith without works is dead,

so we work by faith in God instead!
Not being proud, but allowing
meekness—that restrained power—
to bleed from the depths of our hearts
and make us who God says we are!
With strength and character,
be an example, take up the cross, and remember,
it's Christ that we are following after!

Sow a seed and meet a need.
Get temperance, which is the same as getting self-control.
Beat the flesh under submission
and follow after the Great Commission!
Go! And make disciples, baptizing them
in the name of the Father, the Son, and the Holy Spirit,
teaching them
to observe all that Jesus commands—
everywhere that they will go, everywhere that their feet will track,
in this distant yet familiar land!

Sow a seed bountifully! Love, joy, peace,
long-suffering, gentleness, goodness, faith, meekness,
and temperance—
the fruit of the Spirit is ample and plenteous,
free to give, freely received.
Sow a seed and meet a need!

Written by LmHt and Roy Swan

"I'm the Good Shepherd"

I have planted men over my flock, to care of them as they ought.
To give them love and to help them to grow,
and to teach them how to depend upon me (God), you know.

I say woe to the shepherd who dress so fine, and teaches lots of
untruth, which is blowing my sheep's mind. Woe to the shepherds
who are feeding yourselves, instead of feeding my sheep.

My flock became prey, my flock became meat, you shepherds don't
care, you have plenty to eat.
You eat the best food, you wear the finest clothes,
but you, shepherds, let my poor sheep run to and fro.

You don't care for the sick, you don't care for the weak, you don't
even go looking for my least lost sheep.

I'm looking down on you, shepherds, from heaven above.
You haven't been feeding my flock on the promises
of my love.

I'm the Good Shepherd. I came to seek and to save
all of my sheep that have gone astray.
I'm the Good Shepherd. I came that you might live.
I died on the tree to pardon and forgive.
I'm the Good Shepherd, and on the third day I arose
for all the world to see.

I came that you might live. I arose that you might forgive.
I'm the Good Shepherd. I love my sheep, and my sheep love me.

I'm the Good Shepherd. I'm coming back for my own.
Woe to the one who's not ready to come home.
I'm looking down on you, shepherds, from heaven so high.
You know you'll have to face me (Jesus) one day
in the sweet by-and-by.

John 10:28, End Song: "Gentle Shepherd"
Written by Shirley Jean Foster
December 8, 1986

What Happened

What happened to the days when people use to speak?
The days when you got a smile and a hello from a total stranger
on the street.
The days when it was common and you weren't so overwhelmed,
just to hear a young person say, "Yes, sir," or, "Thank you, ma'am."
What happened—was it something that we did?
Why aren't moral values instilled in today's kids?
Where did we go wrong, and when did we get off track?
Was it when we started letting Little Johnny get away with talking
back?
Just because when Johnny comes through the door, he has to
duck his head,
that's no reason to be intimidated or get scared.
Even though he may be tall and wear size 13 shoes,
as long as he's under your roof, then he should abide by your rules.
Somehow things have gotten out of control.
Could it be some young people don't have no set goals?
Can you imagine them when they are old and gray,
pants sagging, listening to rap music, saying, "That used to be
a hit back in the day."
Maybe they are putting something in the food,
or just maybe it's because they have taken prayer out of the schools.
In today's schools, it's such a shame,
the One person you can call on in time of trouble, they don't
want you to mention His name.
Inside today's public schools, I was surprised at what I saw—
detectors, because I guess that's the law.
Therefore, I would like to challenge each and every one of *you*,
to tell some young person about the love of God because
that's what He wants us to do.

By Roy Swan

Come Out of Sorrow

Woman of today, are you living for tomorrow?
Has your beauty turned to ashes, your joy
into sorrow?

Because of lies and alibis
and all that you could gain,
you left the truth and found out that all was gotten in vain.
Now you're
cussing and you're fussing; your whole life's a strain.
Everything's been emptied,
your heart and soul is drained!

Hold up, wait a minute…
Jesus is the same
yesterday, today, and forever.
He has borne our shame.
Now there are some women of the Bible
who can testify this *thang*.
If they were here, present today, I'm sure you'd
hear them say,

> "I am Rahab, the prostitute whose whole life has been changed! My heritage, my lineage, my DNA is Him, who was, is, and ever will be the greatest man of men. But He's more than just a man. He's King of kings, Lord of lords, Savior of the world. He has given me beauty that I know I didn't deserve. Forgiveness breaks my stony heart, as I submit in love. Up from ashes, I have risen. Awake, I sink no more! Jesus, He's my Lord and Savior. In this, I will rejoice!"

"Listen, Rahab,
I'm the woman at the well,
and I've got a story that I've gotta tell.
About that man who's more, He's more than just a man.
He's creator of the world, He's the great I Am!
He took away my shame
and gave me a garland of praise,
so now I'll stand tall, and I'll tell 'em all,
even the sinful woman with the alabaster jar!"

"Well,
I'm the woman with the alabaster jar.
I'm the one who dared to come into the
Pharisee's house.
They thought I wasn't fit, and yeah, they
were right, but I had to get there,
I didn't care
what they had to say.
Holding my alabaster jar tight in my hands,
I fell to my knees, I didn't have a plan.
Out poured my oil, out poured my tears.
Kneeling in deep contrition,
I washed the Master's feet, and I dried 'em with my hair.
I felt His eyes pierce my heart,
I know He saw my fear,
but my need outweighed my fear,
and it was then right there,
Jesus pulled me up out from the muck of sin.
Old things are passed away, and oh, the new begins.
Out from ashes of despair,
I can help the adulteress woman caught in her affair."

"Yeah,
I was caught in adultery, all my accusers were there.
They threw me down on the ground,
where I lay afraid to get up, I dared not look around,

but then I heard the voice of Jesus, a glorious mighty sound.
He spoke to all of my accusers who held their stones,
ready, aimed, about to fire—the target
was my head.
They were going to kill me dead! Until
the Master said,
'He who is without sin…'—and none could pass that test.
And as He finished with, 'Cast the first stone,'
all my accusers left!
But they left Jesus, and it was Jesus and me alone,
and at that very moment, out from ashes,
a brand-new me was born.
Woman of today, don't wait until tomorrow
to come up out of ashes, to come up out of sorrow.
Our lives are one to coincide.
You ain't so good, I ain't so right,
but Jesus has the answer,
He's the One who lifts us up from filth, dirt, and ashes.
My ashes have been changed to beauty.
No more fear; I'm bold.
Praises be to Jesus Christ, Redeemer of my soul!"

Written by LmHt

This poem was inspired when Pastor Harvey Rollerson was leading prayer and praise at Westlawn. He shared how wonderful it is to have a friend to share with; he said that there is not a friend like Jesus, for you can snuggle right up to Jesus and lay your head right upon his breast (April 30, 1988).

I Snuggle Up to Jesus

I snuggle real close to Jesus. I laid my head right upon his breast.
I said, "Lord, I'm so tired and weary."

He said, "My child, take your rest."

I said, "Lord, I found you just in time. I need you to give peace to my troublesome mind."

Jesus said, "I was waiting for you to acknowledge
that I'm what you need, so here I am to supply you. Make sure
you take heed.

"So go ahead and snuggle up close and tell me all about your cares and woes. I'll show you how much I care, for in my Word you can live, learn, and grow. For you can rest assured that whenever you need me, I'll be there, for I surely do care."

I said, "Lord, my flesh is awful, and it wants everything it sees. There are times it seems like I can't even put it under subjection, you see. For
     I'm not
real strong, and I need your mercy, grace, and strength to lean on.

"Lord, I need you in the morning, I need you late at night, I need
     you dear
Jesus to make everything all right."

Jesus said, "My child, if you are thirsty,
hungry, or tempted, come unto me. I keep telling you I'm Jesus
    Christ. I will
supply all of your needs."

So I snuggled real close to Jesus. I laid my head upon His breast. I
    said,
"Lord, this load is getting lighter, I believe I can stand this test. Lord,
    for in
your Word, I have found peace, love, joy, and hope for my mind. I
    can thank
you, dear God, because you are so good."

"For the commandment of the Lord
is pure, enlightening eyes. The fear of the Lord is clean, enduring
forever; The judgments of the Lord are true; they are righteous
    altogether."

"When everything goes wrong like it sometimes will, snuggle real
    close to
Me. I'm Jesus Christ. I'll speak, 'Peace! Be still!'"

Jesus said, "Go ahead, my child,
snuggle so close to my breast. When you trust, love, and obey me, I
    promise
you I'll carry you through all of your test."

Written by Shirley Jean Foster

The Things I Saw

As I strolled down the streets throughout the neighborhood,
just looking at all the boarded-up and empty lots where
houses and businesses once stood,
my mind immediately took me way back,
to a time when so many businesses were owned by blacks.
What happened to the days when people of color couldn't wait to
start a business or demonstrate their skills?
When did they fall asleep at the wheel?
And while asleep and thinking things were going to stay like they
always had been,
other ethnic groups were slowly moving in.
Not only did they come into the black people's lane,
but they established businesses in almost everything.
It once was blacks who owned the corner stores, restaurants,
auto shops, and laundromats,
but now the only business they own is selling bottled water and
loose squares out of a pack.
Have blacks given up? Have they thrown in the towel?
If they must buy from other ethnic groups, do they have to do
it with a smile?
It seems they have gotten comfortable and have a certain knack,
to joyfully support businesses in their hoods that don't give
anything back.
But as I strolled through the Latino neighborhoods, I hardly
saw any vacant buildings or boarded-up homes.
What I did see was a lot of businesses and a group of people
supporting and buying from their own.
Keeping their money where it'll do the most good,
among their own people, in their own neighborhood.
So will blacks ever get it together? Will they as a people ever learn?
Will they ever get to a point in life of sharing and caring
without expecting something in return?

Now I know we serve a mighty God that is all-knowing, all-powerful, and never needs rest.
But I can imagine when He look at people of color, He must be saying to Himself, "What a mess."

Written by Roy Swan

Seven Last Words of Jesus Christ

For God so loved the world, He gave His only son.
He came unto His own, but God must've known—
the world would not receive the love that He has shown.
The Lord of glory was betrayed by the people He had made.
After they had mocked Him, they continued in their wrong.
After they had beaten Him, they decided He should be hanged.

Hanged between two thieves,
one of whom wanted the Lord to set him free.
He didn't want the punishment—death on a tree.
The crowds had mocked the Lord of glory.
This thief, mocked some more.
But the other smote his breast.
He knew the sins that they committed
were deserving of this death.
He also knew that after death, the judgment had to come.

How could they stand in the presence of a holy God,
without the blood covenant made possible through the Son?
And Jesus in spite of all the wrong,
He suffered for me, for you.
He was beaten, wounded, smitten, afflicted, and bruised,
until he was black and blue,
but He still prayed, "Father,
forgive them for they know not what they do." (1)

The two thieves witnessed all of this. The one who could
only see
Jesus as the possibility, the key for his release,
said,
"If you're the Son of God, as you claim to be,
then why don't you come down off that cross, and take me,
'cause I wanna be free?"

The other shook his head in shame, shame for both of them,
and said,
"Why don't you leave Him alone? We have done our dirt,
but He has done no wrong."
Then he turned his eyes on Jesus,
acknowledging Him as the kingdom that should come,
for he knew this man must be God's holy Son,
and so being thus, he said, "Lord,
when you come into your kingdom, please remember me.
In other words, I know that I'm a wretched soul undone."

And Jesus turned and spoke these words to this peculiar one,
"But be assured these words are true, for all who die in Christ,
to the simple, to the wise:
'Verily I say to you, today shall you be with me in paradise.'" (2)

The people from afar had gathered near and hovered round about.
Jesus saw His mother and the disciple that He loved. As He looked out
into the crowds, they were there, gathered together, and standing side
     by side.
So Jesus spoke these words to them with love and concern:
"Woman, behold your son."
And to the disciple: "Behold your mother." (3)
For He knew in time to come they would need each other.
For if they killed the Lord of glory, what would they do
to those who follow?
Proclaiming hope in Christ,
beyond this dying, sinful world and this state that we call life!

And truly the mother and the son were amazed at His concern
while hanging on a cross for something He hadn't done.
He still cared enough to connect them in His love.
While they pondered on these thoughts of kindness and humility,
they prayed for strength from above.
'Cause Jesus was suffering and bleeding, His body was being torn,
with nails in His hands and a head full of thorns.

He blurted out these words to His Father—
he had no particular fashion, and he had no fancy form—
with a loud cry and possibly a plea,
"My God, my God, why hast thou forsaken me?" (4)

Oh, what pain and agony the Son must have borne,
when the presence of His Father left Him all alone.
I can imagine the heavenly host. I can feel the awe,
the sadness, the sorrow, and the tears that musta' had to fall.
For the first time ever, the Father had to depart
and leave His loving Son to bear the rugged cross.

Jesus realized He was the sacrifice.
The Lamb of God, slaughtered and offered
for the sin of the world.
And there He was, hanging on a cross,
trying to hold His body up.
His human nature must have taken its place,
as He cried, "I thirst!" (5)

The body that He had put on was coming to an end,
so Jesus cried out again, "It is finished." (6)
All the sins of the world were laid upon Him.
His last words were spoken, deliberately and long:
"Father, into your hands, I commend my Spirit." (7)
And Satan thought he'd won...

The sky was darkened, the thunders roared,
the lightnings clapped, the earth began to quake.
Nature knew it could not hold the Savior in this place.
Jesus rose from the dead, went back up to His home,
seated down beside His Father on His mighty throne.
There He waits patiently 'til time for His return,
when
the trumpet will sound, the dead will rise.
We'll be changed in the blink of an eye.

We'll be caught up with our Savior.
Ever to live and never to die.
This is our hope, our peace, our life,
bought by *the blood of Jesus Christ!*

Written by LmHt

The Writing on the Wall

Back in the Bible days, there was a king who was not humble but had a hardened heart.
He did what was wrong in the eyes of God.
Besides being a king that was weak,
he liked to drink, and he liked to eat.
One night he had a big party, and there was lots of noise.
The king got drunk and made a bad choice.
Because way before his daddy got old,
he went to a temple in Jerusalem, and some gold cups he stole.
While he was partying with some friends and all,
he saw a hand writing something on the wall.
The king got scared and was beside himself.
His knees started knocking, almost scared him to death.
So they went and got Daniel up out of his bed,
to come and tell them just what the message said.
Although it was late and way past midnight,
Daniel was a man of God who did what was right.
Daniel told the king that the writing he saw upon the wall
was a message from God, saying his number had been called.
And because of his many sins,
his reign as king had come to an end.
The words that Daniel spoke came true and was fulfilled,
because that very night, Babylon was captured, and the king was killed.

Written by Roy Swan

This poem was written for my sister Brenda, who had to do a poem on spring while she was in college.

(Read with background music, "How Great Thou Art," played softly.)

Spring

When I think of spring, you see,
a magnificent and marvelous feeling comes over me.
I want to jump, shout, and sing, to let the world know
that it is spring.

It's spring! It's spring! I feel great.
The animals come out of hibernation, the beautiful birds begin to sing,
the trees that were dead start to bud again.
The grass is now a wonderful green.
Oh, don't you just love this season called spring?

The earth is the Lord's and the fullness thereof—the world and all
    who live in it.
The Lord knew what he was doing, you see,
because I'm sure spring reminded Him of me.

Spring gives me such a great and glorious thrill, you know,
that often I admire the wonderful pleasure on the different faces that
    I meet,
while I'm walking along these busy streets.

It's fresh, it's clean, I just want to sing.
Hey, world, it's spring!

March 24, 1987

Written by Shirley Jean Foster

What Is Man?

The scriptures tell us that when a man finds a wife, he finds a good thing,
but I don't remember reading what she finds when she finds a good man.
Aren't men just as equally good?
Especially if they are doing all the things that a good and godly man should.
But some women feel that all good men are taken,
and the only ones left are those who just want to lay around,
while she works and brings home the bacon.
A famous singer once said, "This is a man's world," but a lot of people just laughed and thought he was playing,
but ended up missing exactly what this man was saying.
You see, just before God sat down and said that His work was finished,
He took the time to craftily create man in His very own image.
He created him strong, intelligent, and with a moral responsibility to not give up, not give in, and never quit.
Talk about a masterpiece. This is what God equipped man with.
There are some weak men that don't know their role or the power they possess.
That's why some women wear the pants, and the men end up wearing the dress.
This gives women low opinions about men, which explains some of the things they do.
But this is not how God looks at men and women. Neither should you.
Men were created to be leaders, to provide, and to protect.
God gave them dominion over every creature of the earth, and they deserve your utmost respect.
Sure, some men lose focus and forget their role in life.
That's why God created that good thing they're supposed to find in a wife.

But if man is fortunate enough to find that special someone, besides God, who will always put him first, then he will have that peace and happiness he seek, right down here on earth.

Written by Roy Swan

Healed, Set Free, and Delivered

Healing's where I am—healing for the sick, healing for the blind.
Healing hard hearts, broken hearts, bruises, contusions, confusions,
    allusions—
He heals all those
who call out to Him.
Hemmed up, pent down, crushed,
cornered in, stressed out, pressed so hard,
YOU can't make out who you are.
Abused, hurt, misused so much,
YOU can't make out what's real, what's fantasy, and what's just plain lust.

We're making right out to be wrong and wrong out to be right.
Mistaken information, missed the mark, blinded, no sight.
Healing, that's what I'm trying to tell you about.
A Man who can set free, deliver, set free, deliver, deliver, set free me.

Healing, that's the children's bread.
Arise, black children, fight back, live.
Come out from amongst the destructive forces killing your future and
wantin' you dead.
Don't stop being, but stop those beings with prestige and power
who seem to hold the very hour in between.
If I make it or become sour
by what they can offer.
They use their power to change my day into night.
In a second that seems like an hour, the darkest hour
because I'm mesmerized by the mighty, mighty dollar.

MONEY, it's said to be the root of all evil. No! It's the love of money.
Wantin' it all, NOT a little—loads of power, temptation,
having the world at your beck and call, but the end result
Ah, I don't think you want that at all. For
what does it profit to gain the world and lose your very soul
and forever be in turmoil.

Set free, delivered, set free, delivered,
delivered from my dilemma, between making it or not,
because the dollar's in your hand.
You decided my future.
You thought
because you said yes or naw.
"Yes, I'll lend you a helping hand
IF you do what I say you can,"
or, "Naw, not today,
I just don't like you anyway."
Set free, delivered, set free, delivered, delivered, set free from me,
even the likes of me.

Healing's where I am—healing for the lame, recovered sight to the blind.
Set free from sin, set free from death, set free from even me.
Delivered by the deliverer, delivered to live sin-free, delivered from
all these bondages, these things that are holding me.
Sinking ships, a-sinking fast in whirlwinds out of control. In the
        midst of—NO!
Down in the depths of my soul. Set free, delivered, set free, delivered—
that's what He's done for me.

I can tell everyone, anyone, the very first one I see.
I'm set, that's my bread, my portion, my savior has given to me.
Delivered, I've got to be delivered from even me.
Delivered from the blame because of the shame—of all the old things
        I did,
but now I'm happy instead
of crying, trying, scheming, conniving, shucking, and jiving.
I'm set free, set free from me.
Money—shackles.
Getting even—shackles.
Backbiting—shackles.
Greed, the need to succeed—shackles.

Being important, being proud—shackles.
Being light, being bright, even white—shackles.
Long hair—shackles.
Good hair—shackles.
Just not being me—shackled.
Healed, delivered, set free. Set free from even me.

Big nose—shackles.
Bubble eyes—shackles.
Thick lips—shackles.
Big bones—shackles.
Shackled down—bondage.
Bound up—cords.
Wicked bands—strings.
Tied up, sideswiped, NOW has blinded me.

Dark skin—shackles.
Nappy head—shackles.
Big butt—shackles.
All these chains of heritage,
surrounding, swimming, sinking, drowning,
choking the life from me!
Who should I, what should I, who am I to be?
Set free, delivered, Jesus still loving on me.
Set free, delivered, set free, delivered,
delivered, set free from me, even the likes of me.

Healing's where I've got to be. No more walking in carnality!
No condemnation, no more fear, the spirit of bondage is
outta here.
No more laws of sin and death, no more walking in the flesh.
Abiding instead in the Spirit, where righteousness has its
dibs on me.
No more enmity against my God, no more idolatry.
Delivered, set free from strongholds, lies, and vanity.

No more guilt, no more charge, I'm being changed
into the image of God!
And nothing will separate Christ in me! Not death, not life, not even
 principalities.
What once were woes are now deceased.
The blood of Christ cries, "Liberty! I am healed! And set free!
Delivered from evil and delivered from me!"

Written by LmHt

To God Be the Glory

To God be the glory, to God be the praise,
I long for the day to behold His face.
I know if I am obedient and stay in His will,
there's a mansion for me on the top of the hill.
When I think about God and His awesome power,
and all that He has can be ours.

So to God be the glory, to God be the praise,
I promise to serve Him for the rest of my days.
Because He's so patient and because He's so kind,
in spite of our wickedness, He still gives us time.
Time to make up our minds if we are straddling the fence,
to stop living a life like we don't have no sense.

Not realizing that He can satisfy our hunger and quench our thirst,
the only thing He asks is to put Him first.
And why not, back when we had one foot on a banana peel
and the other one in the grave,
God sent His only Son to die in our place.

That was done because after Adam and Eve left the garden,
with heads down and feeling sad,
God told them that life from then on would get pretty bad.
Not just for them, but all people, both young and old,
sin had become a stink in God's nose.
So Jesus had to come to restore our relationship and make
it new,
by suffering and dying for a wretch like me and a wretch like
you.

Written by Roy Swan

Pastor Derrick preached this message on September 15, 2012, at Westlawn Gospel Chapel. This message blessed my heart such that twelve days later, the Lord caused me to write this poem. This message reinforces, in my heart, that God's Word is true and no matter what the situation, circumstances, or problems, God is in control. I could see more clearly how the Lord is working in my life and that God's Word is sufficient. Pastor Derrick's theme for this message was "Hold On, Cheer On, and Church On."

Hold On

I am the way, the truth, and the life, no one come to the Father but
    by me.
Sin entered this world through Adam and Eve.
Hold on, all have sinned and come short of God's glory.
Hold on, if we confess our sins, He is faithful and just to forgive us
and to cleanse us from all unrighteousness.
So hold on,
God in His mighty wisdom and great glory commended His love
    toward us
in that while we were yet sinners, Christ died for the ungodly.
Hold on, when things go wrong like they sometimes will,
and they do not turn out like we think, we should praise God anyhow.
And hold on, when our days are like nights and our skies are not
    bright,
God said it's all right.
Just hold on when your foot almost slips.
Throw your hands in the air like you do not care.
Praise God and hold on,
for His anger endureth but a moment.
Hold on, His favor is life.
Hold on, weeping may endure for a moment.
Hold on, but joy comes in the morning.
Praise God and hold on.

Cheer On, Cheer On, Cheer On

Seeing we are compassed about with so great a cloud of witnesses,
let us lay aside every weight and sin that so easily beset us,
and let us run with patience the race that is set before us.
Cheer on, looking unto Jesus, the author and finisher of our faith.
Cheer on, who for the joy that was set before Him endured the cross.
Cheer on, despising the shame and is set down at the right hand of God.
Cheer on, in God we live, move, and have our being. Apart from
    Him, we can do nothing.
Cheer on, but we can do all things through Him who strengthen us.
Cheer on, bless the Lord, oh my soul, and all that is within us, bless
    His holy Name.
Cheer on, for unto us a child is born.
Cheer on, for unto us a son is given.
Cheer on, the government shall be upon his shoulder,
his name shall be called wonderful counselor.
Cheer on, the mighty God, the everlasting Father.
Cheer on, and the Prince of Peace.
Cheer on, when you toss and turn and can't sleep at night,
God is a shield for you, your glory, and the lifter of your head.
You just cheer on, cheer on.
When God sent Jesus to die on Calvary's tree, he made provisions for
    you and me.
So cheer on, for God so loved the world that He gave His only begot-
    ten Son.
Cheer on, that whosoever believeth in him shall not perish.
Cheer on, but have everlasting life.
Glory to God.
Just cheer on, cheer on, cheer on.

Church On

Oh, give thanks unto the Lord for he is good, church on.

Let the redeemed of the Lord say so, church on.

The Lord is on our side, don't fear what man can do to you, church on.

We will not, do not, cannot give up.

Even though our outward man perish, our inward man is renewed day by day, church on.

How can a young man cleanse his ways? By taking heed of God's Word, church on.

Job said, "Hide me in a grave, appoint a set time, call me, and I will answer to my name." Church on.

Walk in love as Christ has loved us, church on.

The Lord is my shepherd, I shall not want, church on, church on.

The earth is the Lord's and the fullness thereof; the world, and they that live therein, church on.

The water may be deep and the fire may be hot, but hast thou not known?

Hast thou not heard?

That the everlasting God, the Lord, the Creator of the ends of the earth,

fainteth not, neither is weary, church on.

There is no searching of his understanding, church on.

He giveth power to the faint, and to them that have no might he increases strength, church on. The youth will faint and be weary, the young man shall utterly fall, but they that wait upon the Lord shall renew their strength, church on.

They shall mount up with eagles wings, run and not be weary, walk and not faint, church on.

Our family member will let us down, others will disappoint us, many things in this old world just is not fair, but the joy of the Lord is our strength.

Don't look down, look up to Jesus, and church on.

Now unto him that is able to keep you from falling and present you faultless before the presence of his glory with exceeding joy, church on.

To the only wise God, church on.

Our Savior, be glory and majesty, dominion, and power, church on.

Both now and forever, amen, amen. church on, church on.

To our mothers, fathers, sisters, brothers, loved ones and friends,
     elders, pastors,
teachers and leaders, sons and daughters, uncles, aunts, nephews,
     nieces, cousins,
grands and great-grands—to everyone who will read this poem,
be encouraged in Jesus's name, be uplifted and rejoice in the Lord,
and be exceedingly glad and just hold on.

Smile when you don't feel like it, shout if you want to, sing if you must,
but put your faith, hope, and trust
in the Lord of lords and the King of kings who is and was and is to
     come and just cheer on.
Hallelujah! Amen, hold on in the name of our great God and Father.
Hold on.
Glory to God, cheer on.
In the glorious name of the Son, Jesus Christ, cheer on, cheer on,
     cheer on.
Bless God Amen Church On in the name of the Holy Ghost
     Church On
Bless God, for Jesus, He is my Savior, God and Lord, my Keeper and
     Protector.
I will hold on.
Wonderful Counselor, great Redeemer, Son of God, everlasting
     Father, my hope and joy, I will, I shall cheer on.
Praise God, our mighty, mighty Maker, our way out, our shelter in
     the time of storm, roof over our heads, lily of the valley, bright
     and morning star, the light of our salvation, our soon coming
     King, I will, I shall, I must
church on, church on, church on.
Thank God for Jesus, church on.

Written by Shirley Jean Foster

(Scriptures: John 14:6; Romans 5:12, 3:23; Psalm 103:10; 1 John
     1:9; Romans 5:8; Psalms 30:5, KJ)

(Scriptures: Hebrews 12:1–2, Acts 17:28, Philippians 4:13, John 15:5, Psalm 103:1, Isaiah 9:6, Psalm 84:11, John 3:16, KJ)

(Scriptures: Psalm 107:1, 1Chronicles 16:34, Psalm 107:2; 118:6; 119:9-16, Job 14:13, Ephesians 5:2, Psalm 23:1; 24:1, Isaiah 40:28-31, Nehemiah 8:10, Jude 24-25. KJ)

Way Down in the Deep, Deep South

If you could take a trip way back to the deep, deep South,
you just might see a family of seven living in a little old shotgun house.
A house that some referred to as a shack,
a house where you could stand in the front door and see straight
out the back.
A house with a bedroom so small it would make you shake your head,
not to mention three boys sleeping in one twin-size bed.
But if the truth just had to be told,
you wouldn't find no indoor toilet, running water, or gas stove.
What you would find is a man and his wife,
trying to make sure their family had a better life.
Instilling in them the moral values of courtesy and respect,
teaching them that to achieve success is going to take hard work.
Not to expect to get special treatment or get pampered.
But here was a man and father who led by example.
Always up early and ready to roll,
as his wife prepared a hearty breakfast on a wooden stove.
Hogs are oinking, and cows are mooing.
At five in the morning, you could hear that old rooster crowing.
So he pours some water into a pan,
to wash his face and his hands.
He grabs his shoes and slips into a pair of overalls.
You could even hear that old mule kicking in the stalls.
All ready and just rarin' to go,
this old mule's name was Joe.
Now old Joe had a nervous condition and couldn't be still,
and if you didn't keep a firm grip, he would drag you all
over that field.
Let's not forget the children, they helped out wherever they could.
That included feeding the chickens, slopping the hogs, and cut-
ting wood.
The family members weren't the best dressers around.
They often wore what is called hand-me-downs.

To some it seemed like they didn't have much,
but come Sunday morning, they were all in church,
just praising the Lord and giving thanks,
because with God on your side, it's like money in the bank.

Written by Roy Swan

A Mother's Plea for Her Son

Weeks have gone by, days have come,
Lord, I need you to bless my son,
for he needs to come to know the One,
who upholds the world in His hand,
changes hearts, and heals our land.

And those peculiar ones, who will live for you, who will
speak the truth and serve the Lamb.
God of all the universe, God of creation,
God of us,
the One to whom power belongs,
Christ the Savior, God the Son.

Weeks have gone by, days have come.
I wait patiently, faithfully, expectantly
for you to bless my son.
Guide him in the everlasting way,
help him seek Your face
and be found by the One who took his place
on Calvary's rugged cross—He died.
Help him to see, to internalize.

The truth that will make him free,
the way that will lead him every day,
while on earth with its short stay.
The life that will never end, never cease,
so that he, too, will win.
Let him seek all of You
and know Your wisdom,
which is by far a great revelation
of who You are.
Show him Your might, teach him Your love,
and I know he'll be blessed from
heaven above.

Weeks have gone by, days have come.
Give one more blessing,
save my son!

Written by LmHt

"To every thing there is a season, and a time to every purpose under the heaven... A time to kill, and a time to heal; a time to break down, and a time to build up."

(Ecclesiastes 3:1, 3)

Circles have no end, but time does.
Who or what is in your circle?
Did you not know? Have you not heard?
It makes all the difference now and ever, whom or what you will allow into your circle!

CPSIA information can be obtained
at www.ICGtesting.com
Printed in the USA
FFHW021156050319
50866075-56275FF